The Wisconsin Dells

The Wisconsin Dells

A Completely Unauthorized Guide

James Laabs

PRAIRIE OAK PRESS
Madison, Wisconsin

First edition, first printing
Copyright © 1999 by James Laabs

Prairie Oak Press
821 Prospect Place
Madison, Wisconsin 53703

Typeset by Quick Quality Press, Madison, Wisconsin
Printed in the United States of America by
BookCrafters, Chelsea, Michigan

Library of Congress Cataloging-in-Publication Data

Laabs, James, 1952–
    The Wisconsin Dells: a completely unauthorized guide / James Laabs.
-- 1st ed.
        p.   cm.
    Includes index.
    ISBN 1-879483-56-4 (pbk.: alk. paper)
    1. Dells of the Wisconsin (Wis.) Guidebooks. I. Title.
F587.W8L3 1999
907.75'550443--dc21   99-24582
                                                                  CIP

CONTENTS

ACKNOWLEDGMENTS

Researching and writing this book was a labor of love. While I thoroughly enjoyed every moment, it took a tremendous amount of time over the course of almost two years. I'd like to thank my wife, Louise, and daughters Courtney and Carrie, for excusing me on many occasions from my duties as a husband and father to allow me the time needed to take on a project like this.

A great big thank you must go to the many people who agreed to be a part of the research team that gathered information for the reviews found in this book. To review over one hundred lodging places, restaurants, and attractions required the input of many people. I greatly appreciate the time of those who volunteered their opinions.

The photos of Dells attractions and scenery that grace the cover and pages are courtesy of the Wisconsin Dells Visitor and Convention Bureau. Thanks also to the H.H. Bennett Studio Foundation for providing the photo of the famous photographer. And a huge thanks goes to all those folks in the Dells who took the time to talk with me to provide valuable insights into the Dells as well as background for the essays.

Finally, my gratitude goes to Jerry Minnich of Prairie Oak Press, for putting his confidence in me as a first-time author. If I am fortunate enough to have a future in writing, I hope that everyone I meet in the publishing world is as much of a pleasure to work with as Jerry has been.

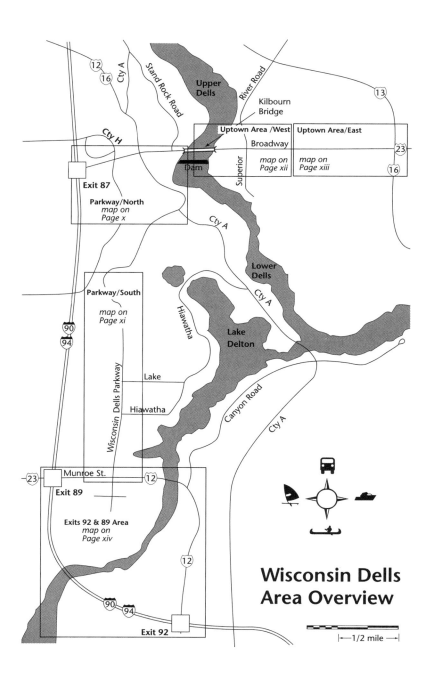

**Wisconsin Dells
Area Overview**

|←1/2 mile →|

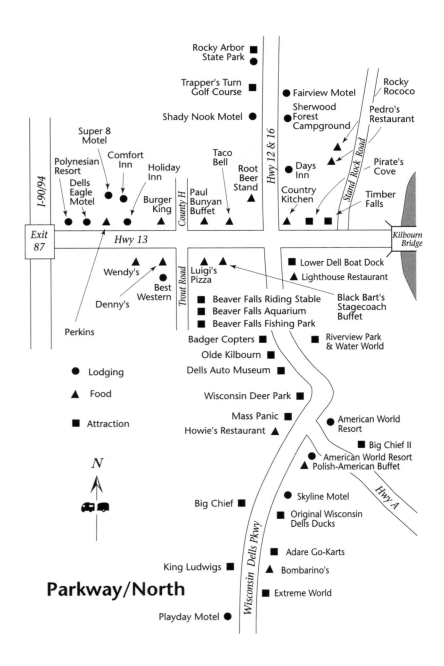

Rocky Arbor State Park ■ ●
Trapper's Turn Golf Course ■
Shady Nook Motel ●
Fairview Motel ●
Rocky Rococo
Sherwood Forest Campground ●
Pedro's Restaurant
Super 8 Motel
Comfort Inn
Polynesian Resort
Holiday Inn
Taco Bell
Root Beer Stand ▲
Days Inn ●
Pirate's Cove
Dells Eagle Motel
Burger King ▲
Paul Bunyan Buffet ▲
Country Kitchen
Timber Falls
I-90/94
Exit 87
Hwy 13
Hwy 12 & 16
County H
Stand Rock Road
Kilbourn Bridge
Wendy's ▲ ▲
Luigi's Pizza ▲ ▲
Lower Dell Boat Dock ■
Lighthouse Restaurant ▲
Denny's
Best Western ●
Trout Road
Black Bart's Stagecoach Buffet
Perkins
Beaver Falls Riding Stable ■
Beaver Falls Aquarium ■
Beaver Falls Fishing Park ■
Badger Copters ■
Riverview Park & Water World ■
Olde Kilbourn ■
Dells Auto Museum ■
● Lodging
▲ Food
■ Attraction
Wisconsin Deer Park ■
Mass Panic ■
American World Resort ●
Howie's Restaurant ▲
Big Chief II ■
American World Resort ●
Polish-American Buffet ▲
N
Big Chief ■
Skyline Motel ●
Original Wisconsin Dells Ducks ■
Hwy A
Adare Go-Karts ■
King Ludwigs ■
Bombarino's ▲
Wisconsin Dells Pkwy

Parkway/North

Extreme World ■
Playday Motel ●

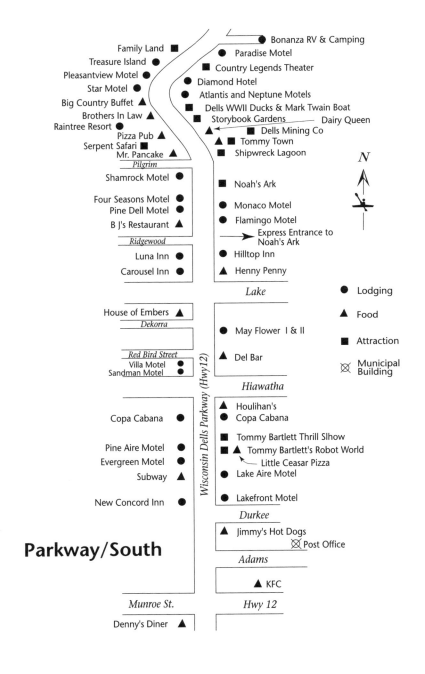

Bonanza RV & Camping

Family Land ■

Treasure Island ●

Paradise Motel ●

Pleasantview Motel ●

Country Legends Theater ■

Star Motel ●

Diamond Hotel ●

Big Country Buffet ▲

Atlantis and Neptune Motels ●

Brothers In Law ▲

Dells WWII Ducks & Mark Twain Boat ■

Raintree Resort ●

Storybook Gardens ■ ── Dairy Queen

Pizza Pub ▲

Dells Mining Co ■

Serpent Safari ■

▲ ■ Tommy Town

Mr. Pancake ▲

Shipwreck Lagoon ■

Pilgrim

Shamrock Motel ●

■ Noah's Ark

Four Seasons Motel ●

Pine Dell Motel ●

● Monaco Motel

B J's Restaurant ▲

● Flamingo Motel

→ Express Entrance to
Noah's Ark

Ridgewood

Luna Inn ●

● Hilltop Inn

Carousel Inn ●

▲ Henny Penny

Lake

● Lodging

House of Embers ▲

▲ Food

Dekorra

● May Flower I & II

■ Attraction

Red Bird Street

Villa Motel ●

▲ Del Bar

⊠ Municipal
Building

Sandman Motel ●

Hiawatha

Wisconsin Dells Parkway (Hwy 12)

▲ Houlihan's

Copa Cabana ●

● Copa Cabana

■ Tommy Bartlett Thrill Slhow

Pine Aire Motel ●

■ ▲ Tommy Bartlett's Robot World

Evergreen Motel ●

Little Ceasar Pizza

Subway ▲

● Lake Aire Motel

New Concord Inn ●

● Lakefront Motel

Durkee

▲ Jimmy's Hot Dogs

⊠ Post Office

Parkway/South

Adams

▲ KFC

Munroe St.

Hwy 12

Denny's Diner ▲

Uptown Area/West

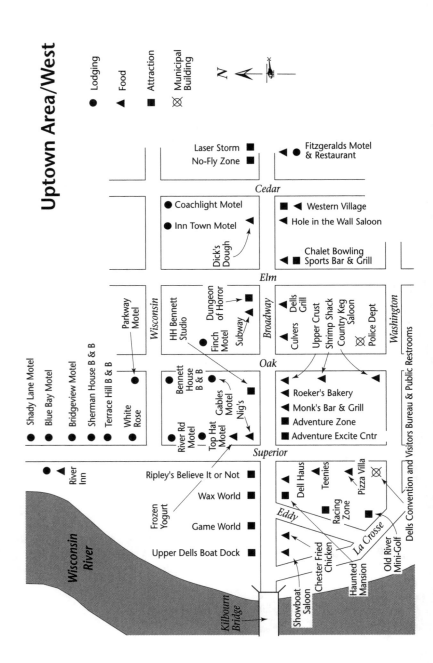

Legend:
- ● Lodging
- ◀ Food
- ■ Attraction
- ⊗ Municipal Building

N

Laser Storm ■
No-Fly Zone ■

Fitzgeralds Motel & Restaurant ◀ ●

Cedar

● Coachlight Motel

● Inn Town Motel

■ ◀ Western Village

◀ Hole in the Wall Saloon

Dick's Dough

Chalet Bowling
◀ ■ Sports Bar & Grill

Elm

Parkway Motel

Wisconsin

HH Bennett Studio

Dungeon of Horror ■

Finch Motel ●

Subway ◀

Broadway

Dells Grill ■

Culvers ◀
Upper Crust ◀
Shrimp Shack ◀
Country Keg Saloon ◀
⊗ Police Dept

Washington

Shady Lane Motel ●
Blue Bay Motel ●
Bridgeview Motel ●
Sherman House B & B ●
Terrace Hill B & B ●
White Rose ●

Bennett House B & B ●

Oak

River Rd Motel ●
Top Hat Motel ●

Cables Motel ●
Nig's ◀

◀ Roeker's Bakery
◀ Monk's Bar & Grill
■ Adventure Zone
■ Adventure Excite Cntr

Dells Convention and Visitors Bureau & Public Restrooms

River Inn ● ◀

Superior

Ripley's Believe It or Not ■

Wax World ■

Frozen Yogurt

Game World ■

Upper Dells Boat Dock ■

Dell Haus ◀

Teenies ◀

Eddy

Racing Zone ■

Pizza Villa ◀ ⊗

La Crosse

Chester Fried Chicken ◀

Haunted Mansion ◀

Old River Mini-Golf

Wisconsin River

Kilbourn Bridge

Showboat Saloon

Uptown Area/East

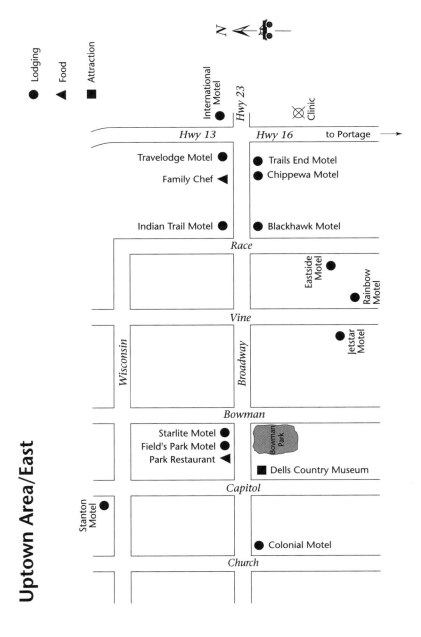

Lodging ●
Food ▲
Attraction ■

N

International Motel ●

Hwy 23

⊗ Clinic

Hwy 13

Hwy 16   to Portage →

Travelodge Motel ●   ● Trails End Motel

Family Chef ◄   ● Chippewa Motel

Indian Trail Motel ●   ● Blackhawk Motel

Race

Eastside Motel ●

Rainbow Motel ●

Vine

Wisconsin

Broadway

Jetstar Motel ●

Bowman

Starlite Motel ●   Bowman Park

Field's Park Motel ●

Park Restaurant ◄   ■ Dells Country Museum

Capitol

Stanton Motel ●

Colonial Motel ●

Church

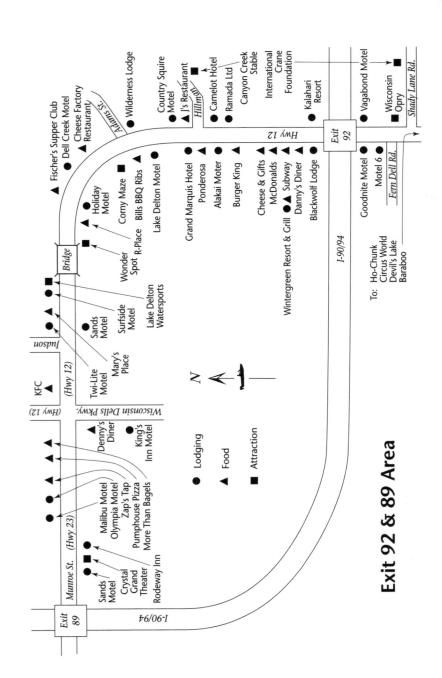

Exit 92 & 89 Area

INTRODUCTION

Why an "Unauthorized" Guide?

This guidebook is intended to be an independent, critical guide to Wisconsin Dells area lodging, attractions and restaurants. The author believes that "the Dells" (the term which this guidebook will use to describe the Wisconsin Dells tourism area) is a fun and exciting place to visit, and that a trip plan based on impartial, high-quality information will make your Wisconsin Dells visit even better.

The Dells can be a confusing and intimidating place. There is a dizzying array of hotels, attractions, restaurants, and shops. A few hours of planning can save many hours of wasted time, reduce family squabbling, and allow you to get the most enjoyment for your time and money.

There is a vast amount of written material about the Dells and its various attractions. However, virtually all of the printed information can be categorized as "promotional." In other words, someone has published that information in an attempt to *sell something, not to inform*. This book is designed to fill the information gap in a critical and unbiased way. If a motel isn't up to par, or if an attraction isn't worth waiting in line for, we can tell you—and as a result save you some money and make your trip more fun.

The author and researchers for this guidebook are not, and never have been, associated in any way with any Wisconsin Dells attraction, restaurant, lodging place, or tourism association. The material in this guide originated with the author and research team, and has not been reviewed or approved by any individual, association, or company associated with Wisconsin Dells tourism.

How Research Was Done For This Book

Nothing was taken for granted in researching this guidebook. Promotional literature from various Dells establishments was gathered and reviewed, but served only as the starting point for the rest of the research. Information was gathered in two ways: First, restaurants, lodging places, golf courses, and attractions were visited personally by the author or members of the research team. These observers conducted in-depth evaluations and rated each place based on certain established criteria. Second, interviews with Dells visitors were conducted to determine their impressions of lodging and restaurants, and to determine which attractions people of various ages enjoyed most—and least—on their visits.

In performing the research, the author and researchers were completely independent and unbiased. If an attraction was visited, regular admission was paid. Meals were paid for, as was lodging at hotels. While the research was planned and rigorous, the researchers looked at the Dells as any visitor would, noting their likes or dislikes of various places.

In researching and writing this guide, the author recognized that a person's age, gender, and special interests very much affect their preference of any particular place to stay, restaurant, or attraction. For instance, an avid golfer would tend to give higher marks to a resort that is adjacent to a golf club than someone whose primary vacation activity is antique hunting. How can fair comparisons be made without taking these factors into account? Obviously they cannot. So, instead of ratings based on any one person's opinion, this book attempts to rate attractions based on the opinions of various categories of people. We selected several groups: families with young children, families with teens, couples, and seniors. But even this approach isn't perfect, because opinions vary with the individual. Two people of the exact same age and gender may rate an attraction quite differently. So, the best advice is this: in planning your Dells visit, review the ratings with your group's ages and interests in mind. But don't necessarily "write off" an attraction before your visit. When you see it in person, it might turn out to be more interesting than you had thought during the planning stage of your trip.

A few disclaimers are in order: Every attempt was made to make this guide as completely accurate and up-to-the-minute as possible, but everything changes over time. You may find a new attraction not included in this edition, or changes in listed attractions. You may discover a new water area at a hotel, or different prices from those stated in this guide. Also, while research was done as thoroughly as possible, researchers can, and do, make mistakes. Given the enormous volume of information gathered and tabulated in preparing this guide, the potential for a few errors certainly exists. The exclusion of any attraction, hotel, or restaurant is unintentional; if a business is not listed in this book, please do not interpret its exclusion as a negative statement about that establishment. Also remember, our ratings are subjective—in other words, they are our *opinions*. You may rate a motel, restaurant, or attraction differently than we did. We welcome your opinions. Simply complete and mail the survey found at the end of this book.

This is the first edition of this guidebook, and your comments, suggestions, and opinions about the Dells are more than welcome. Please address them to: Dells Guide, c/o Prairie Oak Press, 821 Prospect Place, Madison, WI 53703. Again, we encourage you to complete and mail the survey found at the end of this book. Your thoughts will be combined with those of other respondents to help future Dells visitors to better enjoy their trips. Your name, if you choose to provide it, will be completely confidential and will not be used in any commercial manner.

How To Use This Guidebook

This is a complete guidebook for planning your Dells trip. If you're still at home, the lodging section will certainly be of interest, as will sections on attractions and restaurants. If your lodging is already set, the attraction and restaurant sections will still provide plenty of information to help you make the best of your time in the Dells.

But isn't all this reading and planning for a vacation or weekend getaway a little too intense? Isn't part of the fun on a trip to be spontaneous and go where your nose leads you? If you feel that way, you're not alone. But there are about 60 major attractions in the Dells area, well over 100 motel/hotels, more than 20 campgrounds, and countless restaurants and retail stores. You only have so many hours in your vacation and so many vacations in your lifetime. A little time spent reading and planning can help assure that your time and money will be well spent.

Some of the specific benefits of planning your Dells trip are:

(1) You'll be more likely to choose lodging that fits your interests and needs. Do you have kids who love swimming? Are you and your partner seeking a quiet, romantic weekend? The right lodging choice can end up saving you lots of time by being located near the attractions you are most likely to visit and make your visit more enjoyable by providing the activities and atmosphere you want.

(2) You'll save money. Most Dells attractions cost a family of four a minimum of $15 and as much as $90! The information in this guide will let you make a "hit list" of attractions that you definitely want to visit and a "miss list" of those attractions that hold little interest. Planning ahead allows for wise choices, avoiding wasted time and money in seeing attractions that aren't worthwhile.

(3) You'll minimize squabbling among your group or family. Making decisions as a group ahead of time helps avoid last-minute bickering about which attractions to visit. And, if you are well versed on area restaurants, choosing a place to eat at mealtime is lots easier.

(4) You'll save time. We believe it is a misconception that a well-planned trip is too mechanical and/or hurried. On the contrary, planning lets you make the most of your time by doing the things you decide are going to be most enjoyable and skipping the activities that are unlikely to be fun. That leaves more spare time for rest and relaxation.

Traveling To The Dells Area

The Dells area is conveniently located just off Interstate Highway 90-94, about 50 miles north of Madison, Wisconsin. From the Chicago and Minneapolis areas, the Dells is about 200 miles, a solid three-hour drive. From

Rockford or Milwaukee, allow about two hours to drive a little over 120 miles. The interstate highway is usually the best route to the Dells, but alternate routes are available, especially from the south.

Traveling from south of the Dells, one interesting route is: Exit Highway I-90 at the first Madison exit, which is for State Highways 12 & 18 west. Follow 12 & 18 west across the southern edge of Madison. Stay on the road as it turns north. By now, Highway 18 has split off, so you are now heading north on Highway 12. North of Madison, Highway 12 goes through the Sauk City and Prairie Du Sac area. As you approach the Dells area, Highway 12 travels through Baraboo, and within 10 minutes you will enter Lake Delton on Highway 12 at the Exit 92 area. Highway 12 is a two-lane road for much of the distance between Madison and the Dells; the speed limit is 55 mph, and lower in populated areas. This route is about 10 miles longer than the 90-94 route, but may take 20-30 minutes longer due to the lower speed limit. If traffic on I-90 is extremely congested as you approach Madison, however, this route may save some time. If you choose this route, be careful—Highway 12 north of Madison has one of the highest accident rates in Wisconsin.

Another route from the south is useful if traffic on 90-94 is extremely congested. Exit 90-94 at Portage, which is I-39. This is a major exit that splits off to the right. I-39 crosses the Wisconsin River just west of Portage. After you cross the river, watch for the Highway 16 exit and head west. Follow Highway 16 west, which after about 12 miles intersects Highway 13 and Highway 23 at the east edge of the uptown Wisconsin Dells area. Highway 16 is a straight, flat road that follows the Wisconsin River. The river is far enough away and the area wooded enough that it isn't a particularly scenic drive. The speed limit is 55 mph on Highway 16 and police do set up radar in the area. This route can help avoid some traffic jams on the interstate, although many of the delays encountered are often further south.

From the northwest, one idea to avoid traffic on 90-94 is to exit I-94 at Highway 21 east (this exit is a few miles before highways 90 and 94 converge). Then catch Highway 13, and head south through the Adams-Friendship area. Exit Highway 13 at either River Road (in which case you'll take River Road south and end up smack in the middle of the uptown area) or continue past the River Road exit and turn right a mile later to follow 13 as it becomes Broadway.

UNDERSTANDING THE DELLS

A Brief History and Overview of The Wisconsin Dells Area

The story of the Wisconsin Dells begins about 500 million (that's one-half a *billion*) years ago. That was even before the time when the northern part of what is now the state of Wisconsin was covered by glaciers and the Tommy Bartlett Thrill Show put on its first performance. (Just kidding about the last part). Over the eons, the melting glacial waters ran through the Dells area, forming uniquely shaped sandstone deposits. This buildup and the subsequent erosion resulted in the unique rock formations found on the Wisconsin River.

Unique rock formations and unspoiled beauty made the Dells a popular tourist attraction, and good old American capitalism took over from there. Today, attractions and entertainment of many kinds combine with the natural wonder of the area to make the Dells one of the top tourist destinations in the Midwest.

Becoming Acclimated

The Dells area comprises a little less than 20 square miles, and includes two municipalities—the city of Wisconsin Dells and the village of Lake Delton. Sleepy small towns much of the year, they are transformed into bustling tourist areas each summer.

To understand the layout of the Dells area, think of the major tourism area as sort of an elongated letter "C," with the C being about five miles tall. Inside the curve of the C is Lake Delton, a beautiful lake formed by a dam on the Wisconsin River. At the bottom of the C is the village of Lake Delton, with a number of motels, hotels, restaurants, golf courses and some smaller attractions situated on Highway 12. This highway turns north to become Wisconsin Dells Parkway North, the "main drag" of the Dells area. Major attractions such as Tommy Bartlett, Noah's Ark, Family Land, Big Chief's, Riverview Park, and many others line Wisconsin Dells Parkway North (often called the Parkway in this book, often called "the Strip" by locals). You'll also find many motels and eateries on the Parkway. With so much action, the Parkway is one of the major focal points of Dells motor traffic and human activity.

Turn right at Highway 13, cross the Kilbourn Bridge, and you enter the business district, or what many refer to as "uptown Wisconsin Dells." This area represents the top of the "C," and is another center of activity. Here you'll find the most concentrated area of shopping, attractions, restaurants, taverns, and motels, most within easy walking distance of each other.

While the "C" shape is a useful way to think about the Dells region, there are other nearby areas worth noting. Flanking Lake Delton are Hiawatha Trail and Canyon Road, both of which have some waterfront lodging options that should not be ignored. River Road, just north of uptown, also has some nice lodging choices. Highway 13 and Highway 12-16 should definitely not be forgotten, nor should Highway 12 west of the Interstate between the Dells and the city of Baraboo.

Main Areas In The Wisconsin Dells Region

Throughout this book, various areas of the Dells region are referred to. The following descriptions provide a brief overview of each area, plus the major advantages and disadvantages of staying in each.

Exit 92 Area: This area runs along Highway 12 from Exit 92 off Highway I-90 until you reach the intersection where Highway 12 turns north, becoming Wisconsin Dells Parkway North. The Exit 92 area includes some of the most spectacular lodging in the Dells, as well as a number of economy motels and some nice lodging geared toward adults. From this area, a drive of five to ten minutes (in average traffic) is required to reach most major attractions and the uptown area. Traffic on Highway 12 is busy but seldom congested, until the highway turns north and becomes Wisconsin Dells Parkway North. After the turn north, traffic can be a mess. There are several choices in the area for fast food and locally owned table service restaurants.

Advantages: Nearby golf, relatively quiet compared to the Parkway, many restaurants, wide choice of lodging in all price ranges; this is the closest Dells area to the International Crane Foundation, Circus World Museum, and Ho-Chunk Casino.

Disadvantages: You'll need a car to reach major Parkway attractions and uptown.

Wisconsin Dells Parkway: By our definition, the Parkway is the North-South portion of Highway 12, ending at the north end where 12 intersects Highway 13. This three-mile stretch is definitely one of the most "happening" areas in the Dells, packed with motels, hotels, restaurants, attractions—and people. If water parks are your main reason for visiting, the Parkway is the place to stay. Most attractions are either a short or long walk, depending on your motel's location. And that's important, because traffic on the Parkway typically ranges from busy to gridlock. Lodging consists of many motels built in the '50s and '60s, renovated to varying degrees, as well as a few new, spectacular hotels.

Note: Some addresses on the East-West portion of Highway 12 before it turns north refer to "Wisconsin Dells Parkway South." For the sake of clarity, this book uses the terms "Wisconsin Dells Parkway" or "the Parkway" to refer only to the North-South portion of Highway 12, unless citing a published address.

Advantages: The Parkway is where the action is, it's easy to walk to many attractions, and there are many lodging choices.

Disadvantages: Heavy car traffic (crossing the Parkway is a nightmare for pedestrians), atmosphere is anything but tranquil, and the area could use more fast-food restaurants.

Munroe Street/Exit 89: A little off the main traffic pattern, this area follows Highway 23 from Exit 89 traveling east to the intersection where Highway 23 meets Highway 12. The area consists of a few motels, restaurants, and the Crystal Grand Country Music Theater. Motels in this area are generally a little long in the tooth, but a new Rodeway Inn opened in 1997 next to the Crystal Grand. A short drive or a long walk is required to even the closest Parkway attractions. There are some adequate dining spots within walking distance.

Advantages: Less hustle and bustle than on the Parkway, but still only a short drive from the action. Some motels are convenient to dining places.

Disadvantages: This area lacks the atmosphere of the rest of the Dells.

Exit 87 Area: Situated about one-half mile west of the north end of the Parkway is a cluster of hotels, motels, and fast-food restaurants which we call the Exit 87 area. Lodging choices vary from newly-built economy motels to spectacular hotels with water parks. Traffic is busy but not jammed, and although a good selection of restaurants is close, you may feel more comfortable driving than walking to them because traffic makes the road somewhat difficult to cross. Golfers should note that this area is convenient to Trapper's Turn Golf Course.

Advantages: With nice lodging, and a good choice of restaurants, it's a short drive to uptown shopping and attractions as well as the northern end of the Parkway.

Disadvantages: Driving is a necessity, unless you're really willing to burn the shoe leather.

Broadway Area: The "uptown" area of the Dells features close access to boat tours, shopping, food, arcades, and unique "rainy day" activities. Lodging is mostly limited to motels built in the '50s and '60s, modernized to varying degrees. While some lodging is within a comfortable walking distance to uptown, some motels are a fairly long hike away. Restaurants are mostly local eateries, with a couple of chains represented. Shops carrying tourist-type merchandise are easy to find, to say the least.

Advantages: Variety of activities within walking distance, most compact area for shopping, and the center of nightlife for the Dells area.

Disadvantages: Requires a drive to Parkway attractions, some motels may be a fairly long hike to uptown, has lots of noise and activity, especially at night and even more so on weekend nights.

Don't Ignore These Other Areas: While the foregoing areas encompass most of the attractions, eating places, and much of the lodging, there are some other areas that should not be overlooked. Most require at least a short drive to attractions. Many are waterfront areas with available beaches, boating, and water sports.

Close to uptown, *River Road* consists of several motels and bed & breakfasts, some of which have nice views and are located a short walk from uptown. As you travel a little further from uptown, River Road has some very attractive, rustic, and quiet lodging places.

Hiawatha Drive winds along the West bank of Lake Delton and has a variety of nice lodging choices, only a short drive from the Parkway.

Across the lake, *Canyon Road* winds along the east bank and also features some good waterfront lodging. Canyon Road crosses County Trunk A and turns into *Hillside Drive*, which has a few more nice lodging choices.

North of Wisconsin Dells on *Highway 12-16*, you'll find numerous campgrounds and a few motels. If water sports are your thing, consider the camping and lodging on *Highway 13* along the Wisconsin River.

About ten miles west of Lake Delton on Highway 12 is the city of *Baraboo*. Here, you'll find more motels, restaurants, shopping (including chain discount stores), and a few sights to take in. Some of the attractions in the Dells area list Baraboo as their location, although most of these are located between the Dells and the city of Baraboo itself.

Budgeting Your Time and Money At The Dells

Driving in the Dells: If you're on a tight schedule, perhaps on a short visit or weekend stay, saving drive time can let you squeeze in another attraction, or maybe just get in a little extra poolside time. Easily the most common time-waster is getting from place to place. Driving on busy thoroughfares during peak traffic times can turn what should be a short ten-minute trip into a forty-minute adventure. The best ways to avoid traffic jams are: (A) Minimize driving by staying at a motel in a convenient area, and then stick to that area as much as possible for touring, eating, and other activities. (B) Stay in a location that's out of the main traffic areas (a resort, campground, or waterfront resort) and don't venture onto the Parkway or uptown more than necessary, instead enjoying whatever amenities your lodging offers. (C) On busy roads, do your driving mostly during off-peak time, which is generally weekdays and weekends before noon. Also avoid the Parkway during the mid-morning, when Noah's Ark opens.

If you do find yourself driving a lot during heavy traffic periods, one helpful idea is to use I-90 as an alternate to the Parkway to travel north and south. Using I-90 is longer in terms of distance, but can save considerable amounts of time and aggravation. For instance, let's say you're staying at the Black Wolf Lodge and have a sudden urge for some mini-golf at Timber Falls at 10 A.M. on Saturday morning. Instead of driving through Lake Delton and turning right on the Parkway, get on I-90 West, leave I-90 at exit 87, and proceed straight. You will have successfully avoided the Parkway during one of the worst times of the week and saved 30 minutes of frustration. Use the maps in this book or other publications to see how I-90 winds past the Dells, and where the exits are located.

Another convenient alternate route is County Trunk A and/or Canyon Road. (The two run parallel, east of Lake Delton for a mile or so, then intersect.) North of the point of their intersection, Highway A crosses the water and heads northwest toward the Parkway while Canyon Road turns into Hillside Drive and turns east). Besides saving time when traffic on the Parkway is heavy, Canyon Road has some nice scenery, lodging, and even a few attractions that you may otherwise overlook. Review the maps to see how Canyon Road and County Highway A can save you driving time.

Planning visits to include multiple nearby attractions (we call this the park-and-walk strategy) is a good way to minimize driving time. With a little planning, a family can spend the better part of a day in one area and visit a number of attractions within convenient walking distance of each other.

Lines and Crowds: Much of the time, especially on weekdays or close to the off-season, lines and crowds aren't much of a concern. But on summer weekends, holidays, and even on some mid-summer weekdays, crowds can hinder your touring. The good news is that lines and crowds tend to follow a distinct, predictable pattern in the Dells, especially on weekends and peak times. Generally, traffic and lines are sparse in the early morning, when attractions first open. They build gradually until about 11 A.M. to noon. There is a major exception to this pattern. On many days, but especially Saturdays, Parkway traffic becomes very congested for about 90 minutes corresponding to the opening time of Noah's Ark. The peak traffic to Noah's Ark is generally from 9 to 10:30 A.M. In the early afternoon, crowds grow much more quickly until most attractions are very crowded by 2 to 3 P.M. On weekends, the Dells is very active until late into the night. Crowds ease off at most attractions after 8 P.M. but remain boisterous. Water parks follow a similar pattern, but the peak crowd is earlier and begins to thin out after 3 P.M. If your goal is to avoid crowds during peak times, visit attractions earlier in the day and save later hours for relaxing around your hotel.

Save Money With Deals: With lodging, attractions, and food selling at relatively inflated costs, finding ways to save a few bucks here and there is a big help. Here are some ways to cut costs:

(1) *Timing your visit:* A good way to save 25% or more on lodging is to visit the Dells during off-peak times. It's important to recognize, though, that some off-peak times are better than others are. Most lodging rates are at their lowest in winter, but there isn't as much to do at that time.

Lodging rates tend to be highest: (a) on Fridays and Saturdays (which can also be complicated by two-night minimum stays that many motels enforce during peak months), and (b) from early June through the second last week in August.

Most lodging rates are lower: (a) Sundays through Thursdays, and (b) in late May, early June, and the last week of August (after most Wisconsin schools have resumed session). During these periods, you may find rates as much as 25% lower than during peak times, and you will still have many choices for activities because attractions are running close to full steam. In our opinion, weekdays in mid-June are the most attractive "bargain" periods for visiting the Dells, when you'll find plenty to do with somewhat lower lodging rates.

The lowest lodging rates are from the end of October through late December, with a little jump in prices starting at the Holidays and continuing through the rest of the winter. There is often no rate increase for weekends during this period.

As you narrow your lodging selections, call to request written price lists from the lodging places you're considering. The lists usually detail rates and seasonal discounts for various accommodations.

It's possible (but certainly not a sure bet) to negotiate a discounted price for lodging during non-peak times. The best method is to show up at the front desk late in the afternoon or early in the evening and ask for their best rate. After they give it to you, ask for AAA, AARP, and any other discounts for which you qualify. Then, politely ask if they will give you another 10% (or whatever amount or percentage you wish to negotiate) off the already discounted price. Remember, this works because you are likely to be occupying a room that would otherwise be left empty. This strategy works best on weekdays, during less than fully occupied times, and in smaller motels where the person at the desk has some degree of authority. During peak tourist weekends, this technique is more likely to get a hearty laugh than a room discount from the desk clerk.

(2) *Buying attraction ticket packages and savings books:* There are a few attraction package deals which offer savings in return for purchasing tickets to multiple attractions. Perhaps the most attractive one is "Passport to Pleasure," which recently has included the Tommy Bartlett Thrill Show, Tommy Bartlett's Robot World, Upper and Lower Dells Boat Tours, Original Wis-

consin Dells Ducks, Riverview Park, Crazy King Ludwig's, Timber Falls, Pirate's Cove, and Noah's Ark. Purchasing a ticket to your choice of two attractions earned a 15% discount, three attractions a 20% discount, and so forth to a maximum of 35% savings for six attractions. In Southern Wisconsin, the "Bucky Book" is a coupon book selling for $35 that includes a pretty good Dells section of coupons, most of which are of the buy-one-get-one-free variety. The Wisconsin Department of Tourism also sells a $15 "Passport" coupon book, containing many Dells discounts, in grocery stores and other retail outlets.

When you enter the immediate Dells area, keep your eyes open for roadside stands that sell package deals for attractions. Stop on your way into the Dells, but don't rush to buy anything until you've had a chance to see the variety of deals offered in the area.

Another recent offer was the "Wisconsin Dells Coupon Book," which for a small charge (as low as $10 plus postage) provided savings for many attractions, mostly in the form of buy-one-get-one-free deals, as well as some limited but worthwhile savings on lodging, shops and restaurants. For information, call Ad-Lit, Inc., at 800-761-5699. Be sure to look at a detailed list of savings before you buy the book, to be sure the attractions are of interest to you.

(3) *Schools, city recreation departments, church groups, and employers often offer reduced price attraction tickets and/or coupons.* Dells promoters flood Wisconsin, northern Illinois, Minnesota, and Iowa with deals on attractions. Check with your local school district office, recreation department office, your church, or your employer's human resources office to see if there are any deals to be had.

(4) *As you're traveling toward the Dells,* stop at state-owned rest stops and visitors' centers to peruse the literature racks. You'll often find savings on attractions or even restaurants and lodging among or inside the pamphlets. Also look for literature racks in restaurants and at your lodging place, usually in the lobby.

A Word About Scary Attractions

In planning activities for groups with small children, be aware that some Dells attractions are a little frightening and may not be appropriate for younger children. Be sure to take some time to evaluate your child's capacity to handle the scarier attractions. The best advice is to be sensitive to a younger child's fears: Don't let them be bullied or "dared' by older children—or even adults—into entering an attraction if they show fear. Respect the child's feelings, and if they do back out of entering an attraction at the last moment, be sure to let them know that their fear is a natural emotion that everyone feels, and restrain the older group members from teasing the younger children about their lack of participation in any activity.

Potentially Scary Attractions

Air Boingo Bungee Jumping—scares most adults too

Badger Helicopters—some potential to bring out fear of flying

Big Chief—some roller coasters may be too much for youngsters

Canyon Creek Riding Stables—horses can be intimidating up close for the first time

Count Baldasar's Haunted Mansion—observe your child's reaction to the public entrance area

Family Land—the speed slides aren't intended for younger children

J.B. Helicopters—slight potential to bring out fear of flying

Laser Storm—it's meant to simulate a battlefield, noisy and ultra-competitive

Noah's Ark—most slides are no problem, but avoid The Plunge and Jungle Rapids speed slides

OK Riding Stable—horses can be intimidating up close for the first time

Olde Kilbourn Amusements—the attraction you may want to avoid is the haunted house

Ranch Riding Stable—horses can be intimidating up close for the first time

Ripley's Believe It Or Not—some rooms are mildly dark and foreboding

Riverview Park and Waterworld—some rides are moderately scary

Skyscraper at King Ludwig's—open gondola and 180-foot height scares many adults, too

Serpent Safari—mild potential to frighten those who are skittish about reptiles

Timber Falls Flume Ride—mild potential to scare younger children

Wax World of the Stars—some pre-schoolers (and others) find wax figures creepy

Coming Soon—New Hotels and Attractions

One of the challenges of writing this book is that the Dells is in a rapid growth phase. New hotels and resorts with indoor water parks are shooting up almost as quickly as corn in the surrounding farm fields. At publication time, we are aware of a few major new projects.

One of the major new hotel/resorts is expected to be *Kalahari*, which is being built at Exit 92 on Highway 12. The resort will feature 300 guest rooms in its first phase, an indoor/outdoor water park complex, and what its developers refer to as "a retail component." The resort is also expected to have a ten-screen movie theater complex on-site, featuring the latest high-back stadium-style seating. A second phase is projected to double the size of the resort to 600 rooms.

Another project is the Ho-Chunk Nation's planned $120 million expansion of its casino to include a 250-room hotel, an indoor water park, and a convention/meeting facility. The resort complex may also include retail shops, a theater, and a championship golf course.

Chula Vista Resort has also recently begun a $5 million expansion that will double the size of its conference facility, enlarge its indoor waterpark, add a 350-foot outdoor waterslide, and add 100 new guest rooms.

The Dells: Rich In Geological History

If you ask geologist Paul Herr for a list of his suggestions of the most interesting attractions in the Dells area, you'll be surprised at his answer. He may very well tell you that one of his favorite places is the rock cliff behind the Shell gas station at the intersection of the north end of Wisconsin Dells Parkway and State Highway 13.

Paul Herr is owner of Time Travel Geologic Tours and Nature Safaris, a company that gives guided tours highlighting the geologic and natural history of the Dells area. Why is Mr. Herr so fascinated by a rock wall? He sees the wall as a portal through time—a way to see into the distant past of the Dells area.

At one time—500 million years ago—the Dells landscape was not a lush wooded area, but was part of a vast desert. In fact, those geologists who believe that the continents drift an inch or so each year will tell you that the Dells was actually located on the equator way back then! Also, the world of one-half billion years ago was barren of vegetation because there was no ozone layer to filter out the sun's deadly rays. Simple vegetation like algae grew only in the oceans where it was protected from the sunlight.

Because there was no vegetation, the wind eroded the land to a much greater degree than we could ever imagine today. The winds were so powerful that they could erode even quartz, one of the hardest rocks in existence. As the quartz eroded into coarse grains and blew in the wind, it formed huge dunes made of quartz sand. If they were around in the same form today, the quartz dunes would be something of a tourist attraction, since they were 500 feet tall and pure white. But no one saw them—humans would not appear on the earth until hundreds of millions of years later.

The quartz dunes were buried over time under soft sandstone, and sometimes covered for millions of years by glaciers and water (remember, 500 million years is a long, long time). The eroding action of ice and water managed to wear away much of the softer sandstone and shift the rocks, transforming the layered quartz dunes into the preserved wonders we see on boat tours, the Time Travel/Nature Safari Tours, and even behind the Shell gas station. Iron and other minerals contained in the water seeping through the ground have colored the once-white rock, but the formations seen today are fossilized versions of the same huge white dunes that were standing 500 million years ago.

Time Travel Geologic Tours and Nature Safaris give visitors a unique and informative look at the Dells area as it was millions of years ago. For more information about these tours, see the attractions section.

LODGING

What To Look For In a Lodging Place

Location: The location of a motel, hotel, condominium, or campground affects you in several ways. Getting to attractions is less time consuming and may be far less aggravating if you are staying nearby. However, there is no single lodging place that is convenient to all attractions. Also, keep in mind that the Dells isn't that huge of an area. If traffic is light, you can drive from uptown Wisconsin Dells to Exit 92 in less than 15 minutes. Lodging near the attraction(s) where you will spend the bulk of your time is especially helpful on a two-day or weekend stay, but for longer stays location should be considered along with other factors. Proximity to restaurants is also a consideration in choosing a lodging place. The location of many motels makes it convenient sometimes to prepare some meals from the room refrigerator and microwave. Fortunately, many motels equip rooms with these appliances. Finally, there is the matter of traffic, which on a pleasant summer weekend builds to near gridlock on the Parkway and uptown. If you are planning a pleasant summer weekend in the Dells, it pays to keep mid- and late-day driving to a minimum.

Atmosphere: This is a matter of individual preference and how much money you want to spend. Some people view a motel as a place to hit the sheets at night and little else, while other people want a lot of atmosphere and extras. The choice of lodging is very wide at the Dells. At one end are the no-frills motels that, while most may be neat and clean, offer just the basics. At the other end are spectacular hotels that can be considered attractions in themselves. In between, there is a wide array of waterfront condos, B&Bs, rental cottages, and some very pleasant motels. Many places target families with young children, while others cater to couples and to more mature visitors—and many try to appeal to *all* these groups. Couples and seniors should consider whom they will be sharing the pool and lobby with in making a lodging choice. Again, your personal preferences and budget are the critical factors in choosing the atmosphere that's right for you.

Peace and Quiet: Some motels are quieter than others, and some locations are quieter than others. Generally (but not always), motels on the Parkway are noisier, simply because of Parkway traffic and activity. If you're looking for a relaxing, quiet rest by poolside, you may find the odds are better at motels away from the Parkway. If you're looking for activity, the Parkway is the place to be.

Pool and Water Recreation Area: This is another area of personal preference. If you or your family likes to spend a lot of time in the pool area, this is a major lodging feature to consider. Be aware that the term "water recreation area" is used loosely by some motels in promotional literature. Sometimes it means a decorative statue and one water slide, or a small, ankle-deep pool for kiddies. In other cases, it means a full-blown mini-water park with several waterslides. Our research team made brief comments about various water recreation areas, and we list our vote for our top water activity areas elsewhere in this book. But if this is a key feature to you, be sure to ask for more information before making a reservation.

Waterfront Location: Pools are one thing, but if boating, fishing, other water sports, or a water view are important to you, there are many suitable motels, hotels and condominiums from which to choose. In many cases, waterfront lodging tends to be more rustic than lodging in other areas. It's a trade-off—you give up a little urban ambience in exchange for a nice waterfront view. Waterfront lodging usually requires a 5 to 15 minute drive to get to attractions.

Play Area: Many places offer play areas, some more elaborate than others. If this is an important consideration, ask the reservation clerk on the phone to describe the play area: How many pieces of equipment are there? Where is it located on the motel grounds?

Picnic Area: If you are traveling in a large group, or several families are traveling together, you may want to cook together and have a common area for dining. Many motels have modest picnic areas consisting of a table or two and perhaps a grill. Others have covered areas with several tables and grills. If this feature is important to you, be sure to ask the reservationist for details and location of the picnic area.

Security: Two main concerns for travelers to the Dells are crime and auto/auto-pedestrian accidents. While Wisconsin Dells and Lake Delton are small towns, the area is frequented by people of all kinds. Break-ins and robberies are rare and the area is generally considered safe, but some crimes inevitably do occur. The best advice is to take the same precautions you would take in any urban hotel or motel. Lock your doors and windows securely, and never open the door without first checking to see who is outside. If you're particularly safety conscious, hotels with interior access to rooms provide additional peace of mind.

Traffic: In the author's opinion, traffic is a very serious concern, especially on Wisconsin Dells Parkway. Traffic on the Parkway often clips along at speeds well over 35-40 miles per hour, just a few feet from sidewalks packed with families with young children. For some reason (and the reason certainly isn't safety), the powers-that-be of the Dells have decided to have hardly any crosswalks or stoplights on the Parkway. It is a challenge to cross the Parkway at almost any time of the day during the busy season. We *strongly* suggest that you keep small children under *very* close supervision when walking along the Parkway, and *never* allow children to attempt to cross without an adult, especially during busy times.

Refrigerator and Microwave Oven: Many places offer rooms with a refrigerator and microwave oven. If this is important to you ask the reservation clerk. Given the scarcity of restaurants, especially fast-food places, near many motels, it isn't a bad idea to have food preparation facilities in your room.

Condition and Cleanliness of Room and Furnishings: Since many motels in the Dells are vintage 1950s and 1960s, how well a motel is maintained and how frequently it's updated is important. The good news is that because the competition is so intense, the majority of hotels and motels—even the older places—tend to be well kept and at least somewhat updated.

Other Amenities to Look For: *Television.* Almost all area motels have, at minimum, cable TV, and most offer a free pay channel, but if this is important to you, it pays to double-check when making your reservation.

Game room. Many motels have at least one or two video games, and some have more elaborate game rooms.

In-room whirlpool tubs. This option is becoming more popular, so ask the reservation clerk about cost and availability

Suites, large rooms, and cottages. There are many configurations of rooms which can accommodate a couple to a multi-family group.

Explanation of Hotel/Motel Ratings:

(1) *Area* indicates general location. This is helpful in determining if lodging is in the area in which you will be spending the most time. Also, some areas (like much of the Parkway) are bustling, while other areas (such as Highway 12 near the Interstate) are a little quieter. See "Main Areas of the Dells" (page 6) for descriptions of the major areas.

(2) *Water recreation areas* are pools with slides and other water activities located on the motel grounds. While many motels claim such an area, some are true mini-water parks while some others consist of one small slide and a statue. The author's comments are listed for those motels that have a water recreation area.

(3) *Play areas*. Please note that play areas and picnic areas vary widely. If this feature is particularly important to you, inquire about specifics when you call for pricing and reservations. Good questions to ask: How many pieces of playground apparatus are there? Where is play area located? (We observed one motel that had a pretty nice playground—but it was located about 30 feet from a busy road, with no fence or barrier) How many picnic tables? Is there a roof over the picnic tables?

(4) *Room access.* Whether the motel/hotel has interior or exterior corridors is noted. Many motels, especially older ones, have been built in stages and the older sections have exterior room doors and the newer sections have interior corridors. If you consider this feature important, it pays to verify at reservation time the type of access for your particular room.

(5) *Author's Rating:* This is the author and research team's rating of the motel/hotel. The ratings are defined as follows:

☆☆☆ Excellent accommodations with superior atmosphere, activities and visual appeal.

☆☆ Good to very good accommodations with pleasant atmosphere and visual appeal.

☆ Acceptable accommodations, good value but not outstanding in atmosphere and visual appeal.

Obviously, a higher price tag—in some cases, *much* higher—goes along with those places with a rating of two and especially three stars. We found a one-star rating to represent a good, well-maintained place to sleep and spend spare time, but lacking the extra and sometimes spectacular features of the two- and three-star establishments.

(6) *Appeal to kids, couples, and seniors* addresses the important issue of different needs among different groups. Some motels have great kid appeal— a nicely landscaped pool, play area, proximity to attractions, game room, and perhaps a water recreation area are some features that raise kid appeal. These same features turn off many seniors who might prefer relative quiet, nearby restaurants, rooms which are easy to get to, and a high level of security. Couples often look for nice atmosphere, availability of in-room whirlpools, and a quiet environment, combined with a convenient location. Ratings are as follows:

☆☆☆ Very high appeal to that group

☆☆ Good appeal for that group

☆ Lesser appeal to that group

(7) *Nearby attractions* attempts to provide a general idea of proximity to certain attractions. Traffic in the Dells, especially on the Parkway, ranges from busy to gridlock, so being within walking distance of key attractions makes sense. There are trade-offs to convenience, however. The motels on the Parkway tend to be rowdier, kid-filled, and crowded, while some other areas are quieter, with much easier access to a wider choice of eating places. And, motel pamphlets and tourism information aside, there is no one motel that has a location near *all* the major attractions.

(8) *Price range* is intended to provide a general idea of comparative prices. The range includes five levels: economy, inexpensive, moderate, expensive, and luxury. Price may include more than one rating, because Dells motels

often have a wide range of accommodations, often ranging from your basic room with double bed to fancy suites with multiple bedrooms. Also, many motels have price variations based on the day of the week and the season. For these reasons, it is impossible to list exact prices. As a rough gauge, an *inexpensive* rate would be for a basic bedroom with double bed, and an *expensive* rate would be for a suite, cabin, and/or whirlpool-equipped room. The price ranges given should allow you to narrow down your choices sufficiently to choose a motel with only a few calls needed to verify exact rates.

Pricing: economy = low, around $50 or less
          inexpensive = about $50 to $80
          moderate = about $80 to $120
          expensive = about $120 to $180
          luxury = high $180 to $200 or more

Note: All prices are for summer season unless otherwise noted. Winter rates may be lower.

Alakai Hotel & Suites

1030 Wisconsin Dells Parkway South (Highway 12)
608-253-3803
Area: Exit 92, Highway 12 East
Swimming: Indoor and outdoor pools
Water Recreation Area: No
Kiddie Pool: No
Play Area: Small
Picnic Area: Small
Corridors: Interior
Author's Rating: ☆☆
Kid Appeal: ☆☆1/2
Couples Appeal: ☆☆1/2
Seniors Appeal: ☆☆☆
Quiet/Active/Busy: Quiet
Nearby Attractions: Golf
Price Range: moderate to luxury
Comments: Fairly new, clean, adult atmosphere, convenient to a number of restaurants.

Aloha Beach Resort & Suites

1370 E Hiawatha Drive
608-253-4741
Area: Hiawatha Drive & Cty Trk A
Swimming: Indoor and outdoor pools
Water Recreation Area: Outdoor beach
Kiddie Pool: Yes, outdoor
Play Area: Yes
Picnic Area: Yes
Corridors: Mostly interior
Author's Rating: ☆☆1/2
Kid Appeal: ☆☆1/2
Couples Appeal: ☆☆☆
Seniors Appeal: ☆☆1/2
Quiet/Active/Busy: Quiet to Active
Nearby Attractions: Beach and free canoes and paddleboats, short drive to attractions
Price Range: moderate to luxury
Comments: Our favorite waterfront hotel/motel in Hiawatha Drive area. Excellent choice for couples.

Ambassador Inn (Best Western)

610 Frontage Road South
608-254-4477
Area: Exit 87
Swimming: Indoor and outdoor pools
Water Recreation Area: No
Kiddie Pool: Yes, nice kiddie water activity area
Play Area: No
Picnic Area: Yes
Corridors: Interior
Author's Rating: ☆☆1/2
Kid Appeal: ☆☆
Couples Appeal: ☆☆1/2
Seniors Appeal: ☆☆1/2
Quiet/Active/Busy: Quiet to Active
Nearby Attractions: Short drive to uptown and the Parkway, near Trapper's Turn Golf Course
Price Range: moderate to luxury
Comments: Suitable for families, and location and facilities make it an excellent choice for couples and seniors.

American World

400 County A & Highway 12
608-253-4451
Area: North Wisconsin Dells Parkway
Swimming: Indoor and outdoor pools
Water Recreation Area: Advertised as an outdoor one but very modest
Kiddie Pool: Yes
Play Area: Yes
Picnic Area: Yes
Corridors: Mostly exterior
Author's Rating: ☆☆
Kid Appeal: ☆☆
Couples Appeal: ☆☆
Seniors Appeal: ☆☆
Quiet/Active/Busy: Active to Busy
Nearby Attractions: Riverview Park, Big Chief, and other attractions are within a close walk
Price Range: inexpensive to expensive

Comments: A cluster of motels and an RV camp area with a wide range of prices, is convenient to north Parkway attractions and has one of the more unique Dells restaurants, a Polish-American buffet, on the grounds.

Arrowhead Resort & Campground

(Camper cabins, campground, trailer rental)
4179 Highway 13
608-254-7344
Area: a few miles northwest of Dells off Highways 12 &16
Swimming: Outdoor pool
Water Recreation Area: No
Kiddie Pool: No
Play Area: Yes
Picnic Area: Yes
Author's Rating: ☆☆
Kid Appeal: ☆☆
Couples Appeal: ☆☆
Seniors Appeal: ☆☆
Quiet/Active/Busy: Quiet
Nearby Attractions: Drive to all attractions
On-site services and activities:
Laundry, mini-golf, trails, lodge with snack bar
Price Range: economy to luxury
Comments: Hiking trails, bike paths, tennis courts and shuffleboard available. Listed here as a motel because trailers up to three bedrooms are available for rental.

Artist's Glen Resort

4124 River Road
608-254-2711
Area: River Road
Swimming: Outdoor pool
Water Recreation Area: No
Kiddie Pool: No
Play Area: Yes

Picnic Area: Yes
Corridors: Exterior
Author's Rating: ☆1/2
Kid Appeal: ☆
Couples Appeal: ☆☆
Seniors Appeal: ☆☆
Quiet/Active/Busy: Quiet
Nearby Attractions: Drive to all attractions, restaurant on-site
Price Range: moderate to luxury
Comments: Hiking trails, bike paths, tennis courts and shuffleboard available.

Atlantis Hotel and Neptune's EconoKing

1570 Wisconsin Dells Parkway
608-253-6606
Area: Middle Dells Parkway
Swimming: Indoor and outdoor pools
Water Recreation Area: Yes—indoor is quite nice, outdoor a bit small
Kiddie Pool: Yes
Play Area: Yes
Picnic Area: No
Corridors: Many interior
Author's Rating: ☆☆1/2
Kid Appeal: ☆☆☆☆
Couples Appeal: ☆☆
Seniors Appeal: ☆1/2
Quiet/Active/Busy: Active
Nearby Attractions: Noah's Ark and other attractions are nearby
Price Range: inexpensive to expensive (see comments)
Comments: Atlantis is the higher priced of the two, but offers more amenities than Neptune's. Both have access to water recreation and are located convenient to attractions.

Aztec Motel

425 S Vine Street
254-7404
Area: Off-Broadway

Swimming: None
Water Recreation Area: No
Kiddie Pool: No
Play Area: Yes
Picnic Area: Yes
Corridors: Exterior
Author's Rating: 1/2
Kid Appeal: 1/2
Couples Appeal: ☆
Seniors Appeal: ☆
Quiet/Active/Busy: Quiet to Active
Nearby Attractions: Walk to uptown
Price Range: economy to inexpensive
Comments: Tiny motel in small cluster of small motels. There is no pool.

Baker's Sunset Bay Resort
921 Canyon Road
608-254-8406
Area: Canyon Road
Swimming: Indoor and outdoor pools
Water Recreation Area: No
Kiddie Pool: Yes, very nice water play area
Play Area: Yes
Picnic Area: Yes
Corridors: Exterior, condo and cabin style
Author's Rating: ☆☆1/2
Kid Appeal: ☆☆
Couples Appeal: ☆☆1/2
Seniors Appeal: ☆☆1/2
Quiet/Active/Busy: Quiet to Active
Nearby Attractions: Beach, free rowboats, short drive to attractions
Price Range: moderate to expensive
Comments: Very pleasant atmosphere makes this a good choice.

Birchcliff Resort
4149 River Road
608-254-7515
Area: River Road
Swimming: Outdoor pools
Water Recreation Area: No

Kiddie Pool: No
Play Area: Yes
Picnic Area: Yes
Corridors: Cottage style motel
Author's Rating: ☆☆
Kid Appeal: ☆
Couples Appeal: ☆☆
Seniors Appeal: ☆☆
Quiet/Active/Busy: Quiet
Nearby Attractions: Short drive to attractions
Price Range: economy to expensive
Comments: Quiet atmosphere. The outdoor table tennis table made of stone is one of the more unique guest amenities in the Dells area.

Black Hawk Motel
E Broadway and Race
608-254-7770
Area: Broadway
Swimming: Indoor and outdoor pools
Water Recreation Area: No
Kiddie Pool: Outdoor
Play Area: Yes
Picnic Area: Yes
Corridors: Exterior
Author's Rating: ☆☆
Kid Appeal: ☆1/2
Couples Appeal: ☆☆
Seniors Appeal: ☆☆1/2
Quiet/Active/Busy: Quiet to Active
Nearby Attractions: Short distance from uptown
Price Range: inexpensive to moderate
Comments: Nicely maintained, within short walking distance of uptown attractions.

Black Wolf Lodge
Highway 12 and I-90
(PO Box 50, Zip 53965)
608-253-2222
Area: Exit 92
Swimming: Indoor and outdoor pools

Water Recreation Area: Yes—indoor and outdoor, one of the best in the Dells area
Kiddie Pool: Yes
Play Area: Yes
Picnic Area: Yes
Corridors: Interior
Author's Rating: ☆☆☆
Kid Appeal: ☆☆☆
Couples Appeal: ☆☆☆
Seniors Appeal: ☆☆1/2
Quiet/Active/Busy: Active
Nearby Attractions: Golf nearby, a ten-minute drive (in average traffic) to most major attractions
Price Range: luxury
Comments: Built in 1997 by a group including the former owners of Noah's Ark, this is one of the newest, and most spectacular hotels in the area. Very impressive outdoor water recreation area, and indoor area is perhaps the best in the Dells. Room rates are pricey, even in off-season, but Black Wolf Lodge has quickly become one of the most popular hotels in the Dells.

Blue Bay Motel

1026 River Road
608-254-1026
Area: River Road near uptown
Swimming: Outdoor pool
Water Recreation Area: No
Kiddie Pool: No
Play Area: Modest
Picnic Area: Modest
Corridors: Exterior
Author's Rating: ☆1/2
Kid Appeal: ☆
Couples Appeal: ☆
Seniors Appeal: ☆1/2
Quiet/Active/Busy: Active
Nearby Attractions: Walk to uptown attractions
Price Range: economy

Comments: Older, economy motel near uptown. Some larger rooms and cottages available.

Blue Water Condominiums

Managed by Sand County Service Company
608-254-6551
Area: West shore of Lake Delton
Swimming: beach only
Water Recreation Area: no
Kiddie Pool: no
Play Area: no
Picnic Area: yes
Corridors: Exterior
Author's Rating: ☆☆
Kid Appeal: ☆
Couples Appeal: ☆☆
Seniors: ☆☆
Quiet/Active/Busy: Quiet
Nearby: Short drive or long walk to the Parkway
Price Range: Moderate to expensive
Comments: No pools, but nice waterfront location and convenience to the Parkway.

Cambrian Vacation Rentals

PO Box 384, Lake Delton 53940
800-424-4002
Private condominium, cabin, and cottage rentals. This company rents a wide variety of privately owned homes, cottages, condos, etc. Phone to see whether they have what you want, at the price you want to pay.

Camelot Hotel & Suites

1033 Highway 12
608-253-3000
Area: Exit 92
Swimming: Will have indoor and outdoor pools
Water Recreation Area: Yes
Kiddie Pool: Yes

Corridors: interior
Author's Rating: Not yet open at time of publication, expected to be ☆☆☆ with expensive to luxury prices.
Comments: Under construction at time of publication, Camelot will be open by summer 1999.

Caribbean Club Resort

1093 Canyon Road
608-254-4777/800-800-6981
Area: Canyon Road, east shore of Lake Delton
Swimming: Indoor and outdoor pools
Water Recreation Area: Yes, outdoor area is nicely landscaped
Kiddie Pool: Yes
Play Area: Yes
Picnic Area: Outdoor grills available
Corridors: Condo style
Author's Rating: ☆☆☆
Kid Appeal: ☆☆☆
Couples Appeal: ☆☆☆
Seniors Appeal: ☆☆1/2
Quiet/Active/Busy: Active to busy
Nearby Attractions: Boat dock and beach on-site, short drive to attractions
Price Range: expensive to luxury
Comments: Condo-style units with 1-3 bedrooms, full kitchen, and fireplace. Atmosphere is somewhat hectic in season, but still a very pleasant water-front resort.

Carousel Inn and Suites

Wisconsin Dells Parkway at Lake
608-254-6554
Area: South Dells Parkway
Swimming: Indoor and outdoor pools
Water Recreation Area: Yes—outdoor—candy theme will appeal most to small children
Kiddie Pool: Yes
Play Area: Yes
Picnic Area: Yes

Corridors: Some interior, some exterior
Author's Rating: ☆☆
Kid Appeal: ☆☆☆, especially for younger children
Couples Appeal: ☆☆
Seniors Appeal: ☆
Quiet/Active/Busy: Active to Busy
Nearby Attractions: Noah's Ark across the Parkway and other attractions nearby
Price Range: inexpensive to expensive
Comments: Nice play area and strong appeal to younger children.

Christmas Mountain

Condo rentals
S9444 Christmas Mountain Road
Wisconsin Dells
608-253-1000
Area: West of I-90/94
Swimming: Outdoor pool
Kiddie Pool: No
Water Recreation: No
Play Area: No
Picnic Area: No
Corridors: Internal and exterior
Author's Rating: ☆☆
Kid Appeal: ☆
Couples Appeal: ☆☆
Senior Appeal: ☆☆
Nearby: Golf on-site, drive to other attractions
Price: Moderate to luxury
Comments: A bit out of the way, but quiet and pleasant.

Chula Vista

4031 River Road
608-254-8366
Area: On Wisconsin River north of town
Swimming: Indoor and outdoor pools
Water Recreation Area: Yes—outdoor and indoor, with expansion planned
Kiddie Pool: Yes, very nice area
Play Area: Yes

Picnic Area: Yes
Corridors: Many interior
Author's Rating: ☆☆☆
Kid Appeal: ☆☆☆
Couples Appeal: ☆☆☆
Seniors Appeal: ☆☆☆
Quiet/Active/Busy: Quiet to Active
Nearby Attractions: Waterfront
location, very close to Coldwater
Canyon Golf Course, ten minute
drive to most other attractions.
Price Range: moderate to luxury
Comments: A little out of the way, but
good restaurants on premises, and an
interesting place to stay. An expanded
water recreation area is new for 1999.
"Coyote Mountain" will feature ruins,
an Aztec temple, and a kiddie area with
soft, floating toy animals.

Cliffside Resort and Suites

351 Canyon Road
608-254-8521
Area: Canyon Road
Swimming: Indoor pools
Water Recreation: No
Kiddie Pool: Yes
Play Area: No
Picnic Area: Yes
Corridors: Interior
Author's Rating: ☆☆
Kid Appeal: ☆1/2
Couples Appeal: ☆☆1/2
Seniors Appeal: ☆☆1/2
Quiet/Active/Busy: Quiet
Nearby Attractions: Waterfront
location, nearby golf, drive to
major attractions
Price Range: inexpensive to luxury
Comments: Quiet, nice waterfront loca-
tion, high appeal to couples and seniors.

Coachlight Motel

827 Cedar Street
608-254-7917
Swimming: None
Water Recreation Area: No
Kiddie Pool: No
Play Area: No
Picnic Area: No
Corridors: Exterior
Author's Rating: ☆
Kid Appeal: ☆
Couples Appeal: ☆
Seniors Appeal: ☆
Quiet/Active/Busy: Quiet to Active
Nearby Attractions: Short walk
to uptown attractions
Price Range: economy to inexpensive
Comments: Not many frills, but very
close to uptown.

Colonial Motel

606 Broadway
608-254-7771
Area: Broadway
Swimming: Outdoor pool
Water Recreation Area: No
Kiddie Pool: No
Play Area: No
Picnic Area: Yes
Corridors: Exterior
Author's Rating: ☆
Kid Appeal: ☆
Couples Appeal: ☆
Seniors Appeal: ☆
Quiet/Active/Busy: Quiet to Active
Nearby Attractions: Short walk
to uptown business district
Price Range: inexpensive to moderate
Comments: Good location if you plan on
spending a lot of time uptown.

Comfort Inn

Highway 13
608-253-3711
Area: Exit 87
Swimming: Indoor pool
Water Recreation Area: No
Kiddie Pool: No
Play Area: No
Picnic Area: No
Corridors: interior
Author's Rating: ☆1/2
Kid Appeal: ☆
Couples Appeal: ☆☆
Seniors Appeal: ☆☆
Quiet/Active/Busy: Quiet to Active
Nearby Attractions: Convenient to
Trapper's Turn Golf. Most other
attractions are a short drive away.
Price Range: inexpensive to moderate
Comments: Nothing spectacular, but a
nice, fairly low-cost place to stay, espe-
cially for adults.

Copa Cabana Resort Hotel and Suites

611 Wisconsin Dells Parkway
608-253-1511
Area: Wisconsin Dells Parkway
Swimming: Indoor and Outdoor pools
Water Recreation Area: Yes, indoor
and outdoor are attractive
Kiddie Pool: Yes
Play Area: Yes
Picnic Area: Yes
Corridors: Mostly interior
Author's Rating: ☆☆1/2
Kid Appeal: ☆☆☆
Couples Appeal: ☆☆☆
Seniors Appeal: ☆☆1/2
Quiet/Active/Busy: Busy
Nearby Attractions: Convenient to
Noah's Ark, Tommy Bartlett and
many other Parkway attractions
Price Range: expensive to luxury

Comments: Nice feature is skywalk over
Dells Parkway, the best and safest way
to cross this busy street.

Country Squire Motel

831 Wisconsin Dells Parkway South
608-253-1211
Area: Exit 92
Swimming: Outdoor pool
Water Recreation Area: No
Kiddie Pool: No
Play Area: Yes
Picnic Area: Yes
Corridors: Exterior
Author's Rating: 1/2
Kid Appeal: ☆
Couples Appeal: ☆
Seniors Appeal: ☆
Quiet/Active/Busy: Active
Nearby Attractions: riding stable,
must drive to Parkway attractions
and uptown
Price Range: economy to moderate
Comments: Somewhat convenient
Highway 12 location and some OK
rooms, but better economy choices are
available.

D'Amours Big Cedar Lodge

E11232 Hillside Dr
254-8456
Area: On waterfront near County A
Swimming: Outdoor pool
Water Recreation Area: No
Kiddie Pool: No
Play Area: Yes
Picnic Area: Yes
Corridors: Exterior
Author's Rating: ☆☆
Kid Appeal: ☆1/2
Couples Appeal: ☆☆1/2
Seniors Appeal: ☆☆
Quiet/Active/Busy: Quiet to Active

Nearby Attractions: Waterfront location, drive to all attractions, has beach and boat rentals
Price Range: moderate to luxury
Comments: Very nice selection of log cabin style motel rooms and cabins.

Days End Motel

N604 Highway 12-16
608-254-8171
Area: North of uptown area
Swimming: Outdoor pool
Kiddie Pool: No
Play Area: Yes
Picnic Area: Yes
Corridors: Exterior
Author's Rating: ☆
Kid Appeal: ☆
Couples Appeal: ☆
Seniors Appeal: ☆
Quiet/Active/Busy: Quiet
Nearby Attractions: Watersports, short drive to updown
Price Range: Economy to moderate
Comments: Quiet location away from the hustle and bustle.

Days Inn of Wisconsin Dells

944 Highway 12 just north of Highway 13 intersection
608-254-6444
Area: north end of Wisconsin Dells Parkway
Swimming: Indoor and outdoor pool
Water Recreation Area: No
Kiddie Pool: No
Play Area: No
Picnic Area: No
Corridors: interior
Author's Rating: ☆
Kid Appeal: ☆
Couples Appeal: ☆☆
Seniors Appeal: ☆☆
Quiet/Active/Busy: Quiet to Active

Nearby Attractions: Very convenient to Pirate's Cove, Timber Falls, and Trapper's Turn golf, most other attractions are short drive.
Price Range: inexpensive to expensive
Comments: A little bit out of the way on far north end of the Parkway, but a nice, lower cost place to stay, especially for adults. Only a very short walk to restaurants, a few attractions, and shopping.

Deer Trail Motel

1234 River Road
608-254-8535
Area: On Wisconsin River a few blocks from uptown
Swimming: Outdoor pool
Water Recreation Area: No
Kiddie Pool: No
Play Area: Yes
Picnic Area: Yes
Corridors: Exterior
Author's Rating: ☆1/2
Kid Appeal: ☆
Couples Appeal: ☆☆
Seniors Appeal: ☆☆
Quiet/Active/Busy: Quiet
Nearby Attractions: Short walk to uptown
Price Range: inexpensive to expensive
Comments: Cottage-like layout, very well maitained.

Del Rancho Motel

1231 Wisconsin Dells Parkway South
608-253-4561
Area: Exit 92
Swimming: Outdoor pool
Water Recreation Area: No
Kiddie Pool: Yes
Play Area: Yes
Picnic Area: Yes
Corridors: Exterior
Author's Rating: 1/2

Kid Appeal: 1/2
Couples Appeal: ☆
Seniors Appeal: ☆
Quiet/Active/Busy: Quiet
Nearby Attractions: Drive ten minutes
to Parkway attractions
Price Range: economy to inexpensive
Comments: Across Highway 12 from
several fast-food restaurants.

Dell Creek Motel
501 Wisconsin Dells Parkway South
(Highway 12)
608-253-7301
Area: Exit 92, toward town
Swimming: Outdoor pool
Water Recreation Area: No
Kiddie Pool: Outdoor
Play Area: Limited
Picnic Area: Limited
Corridors: exterior
Author's Rating: 1/2
Kid Appeal: 1/2
Couples Appeal: ☆
Seniors Appeal: ☆
Quiet/Active/Busy: Quiet to Active
Nearby Attractions: Wonder Spot,
short drive to Parkway attractions
Price Range: economy to inexpensive
Comments: Economy choice on High-
way 12.

Dells Club Condominiums
Managed by Sand County
Service Company
Area: Hwy. 13 north of uptown
Swimming: Outdoor pool
Water Recreation Area: No
Play Area: No
Picnic Area: Yes
Corridors: Exterior
Author's Rating: ☆☆
Kid Appeal: ☆
Couples Appeal: ☆☆
Seniors Appeal: ☆☆

Quiet/Active/Busy: Quiet
Nearby Attractions: Fishing and
canoeing
Price Range: Moderate to expensive
Comments: A bit out of the way, but
quiet, pleasant atmosphere.

Dells Eagle Motel
833 N Frontage Road
608-254-4505
Area: Exit 87
Swimming: Indoor and outdoor pool
Water Recreation Area: No
Kiddie Pool: Yes
Play Area: Yes
Picnic Area: Yes
Corridors: interior
Author's Rating: ☆☆
Kid Appeal: ☆1/2
Couples Appeal: ☆☆
Seniors Appeal: ☆☆
Quiet/Active/Busy: Quiet to Active
Nearby Attractions: Short drive to
Trapper's Turn Golf and most other
attractions
Price Range: moderate to expensive
Comments: Relatively small and quiet,
clean, in good location for dining
choices.

Dells Gateway Motel
401 Vine Street
608-253-2451
Area: A few blocks off Broadway
Swimming: Outdoor pool
Water Recreation Area: No
Kiddie Pool: Yes
Play Area: Yes
Picnic Area: Yes
Corridors: Exterior
Author's Rating: ☆
Kid Appeal: ☆
Couples Appeal: ☆
Seniors Appeal: ☆
Quiet/Active/Busy: Quiet

Nearby Attractions: A short hike
to uptown
Price Range: economy to moderate
Comments: A little off the beaten track,
but a good value.

Dells Jetstar Motel
725 Vine Street
608-254-4668
Area: A few blocks off Broadway
Swimming: No
Water Recreation Area: No
Kiddie Pool: No
Play Area: No
Picnic Area: No
Corridors: Exterior
Author's Rating: ☆
Kid Appeal: 1/2
Couples Appeal: ☆
Seniors Appeal: ☆
Quiet/Active/Busy: Quiet
Nearby Attractions: Fairly short hike
to uptown
Price Range: economy to inexpensive
Comments: A little out of the way, quite
small, and no pool makes it a poor
choice for families.

Delton Oaks Motel
730 E Hiawatha Drive
608-253-4092
Area: Hiawatha Drive waterfront
Swimming: Outdoor pool
Water Recreation Area: No
Kiddie Pool: No
Play Area: Yes
Picnic Area: Yes
Corridors: Exterior
Author's Rating: ☆
Kid Appeal: ☆
Couples Appeal: ☆
Seniors Appeal: ☆
Quiet/Active/Busy: Quiet
Nearby Attractions: Short drive to
Highway 12 and the Parkway

Price Range: inexpensive to moderate
Comments: Small play area, waterfront
location.

Diamond Hotel
1630 Wisconsin Dells Parkway
608-253-6500
Area: Dells Parkway
Swimming: Indoor and outdoor pool
Water Recreation Area: Nicely
landscaped pool but not spectacular
Kiddie Pool: Outdoor
Play Area: Yes, small
Picnic Area: Yes
Corridors: Many interior
Author's Rating: ☆☆1/2
Kid Appeal: ☆☆
Couples Appeal: ☆☆1/2
Seniors Appeal: ☆☆1/2
Quiet/Active/Busy: Active to Busy
Nearby Attractions: Convenient to a
number of Dells Parkway attractions
Price Range: inexpensive to expensive
Comments: Pleasant and attractive place
to stay on the Parkway, and an easy walk
to many attractions.

Evergreen Motel
461 Wisconsin Dells Parkway
608-254-2666
Area: Dells Parkway
Swimming: Outdoor pool
Water Recreation Area: No
Kiddie Pool: No
Play Area: Yes
Picnic Area: Yes
Corridors: Exterior
Author's Rating: 1/2
Kid Appeal: ☆
Couples Appeal: ☆
Seniors Appeal: ☆
Quiet/Active/Busy: Quiet to Active
Nearby Attractions: Moderate distance
walk to Noah's Ark and some other
Parkway attractions

Price Range: economy to moderate
Comments: Modestly appointed, low-cost place to stay on the Parkway.

Fairview Motel
Highway 16
Area: Highway 16
just North of the Parkway
Swimming: Outdoor pool
Water Recreation Area: No
Kiddie Pool: No
Play Area: No
Picnic Area: No
Corridors: Exterior
Author's Rating: ☆
Kid Appeal: 1/2
Couples Appeal: ☆
Seniors Appeal: ☆
Quiet/Active/Busy: Quiet to Active
Nearby Attractions: Entrance to
Trappers Turn golf course located
directly across highway, not too far
from Pirate's Cove entrance but high-way location necessitates driving to
all other attractions
Price Range: economy to inexpensive
Comments: Modest place to stay, a little
out of the way.

Finch Motel
811 Oak Street
608-253-4342
Area: Uptown
Swimming: No
Water Recreation Area: No
Kiddie Pool: No
Play Area: No
Picnic Area: Yes
Corridors: Exterior
Author's Rating: 1/2
Kid Appeal: 1/2
Couples Appeal: ☆
Seniors Appeal: ☆
Quiet/Active/Busy: Active

Nearby Attractions: a very short walk
to uptown attractions
Price Range: economy to inexpensive
Comments: No swimming but very close
to uptown attractions and restaurants.

Fitzgerald's Motel
530 Broadway
608-253-1651
Area: Broadway, edge of uptown
Swimming: Outdoor pool
Water Recreation Area: No
Kiddie Pool: No
Play Area: No
Picnic Area: Yes
Corridors: Exterior
Author's Rating: ☆
Kid Appeal: ☆
Couples Appeal: ☆
Seniors Appeal: ☆
Quiet/Active/Busy: Busy
Nearby Attractions: All uptown
attractions
Price Range: economy to moderate
Comments: You can't stay much closer
to uptown. Broadway location means
you can expect a lot of hustle and bustle.

Flamingo Motel and Suites
1220 Wisconsin Dells Parkway
608-253-2911
Area: Dells Parkway
Swimming: Indoor and outdoor pool,
nice adult pool separate
Water Recreation Area: Kiddie slide
and nice kiddie area, giant tipping
bucket is entertaining
Kiddie Pool: Yes
Play Area: Yes
Picnic Area: Yes, covered area with
several tables, outdoor grills
Corridors: Exterior
Author's Rating: ☆☆
Kid Appeal: ☆☆1/2
Couples Appeal: ☆☆

Seniors Appeal: ☆☆
Quiet/Active/Busy: Active to Busy
Nearby Attractions: Very convenient
to Noah's Ark and to many other
Parkway attractions
Price Range: moderate to luxury
Comments: One of the most convenient
motels to Noah's Ark, and an excellent
picnic area.

Four Seasons Motel

1231 Wisconsin Dells Parkway
608-253-6641
Area: Wisconsin Dells Parkway
Swimming: Indoor and outdoor pool
Water Recreation Area: No
Kiddie Pool: No
Play Area: Yes, small
Picnic Area: Yes, small
Corridors: Exterior
Author's Rating: ☆
Kid Appeal: ☆
Couples Appeal: ☆
Seniors Appeal: ☆
Quiet/Active/Busy: Active
Nearby Attractions: Convenient to
Noah's Ark and convenient to many
Parkway attractions
Price Range: economy to moderate
Comments: Basic lodging on a conve-
nient part of the Parkway.

Gables Motel

822 Oak Street
608-253-3831
Swimming: Small outdoor pool
Water Recreation Area: No
Kiddie Pool: No
Play Area: No
Picnic Area: No
Corridors: Exterior
Author's Rating: ☆1/2
Kid Appeal: ☆
Couples Appeal: ☆
Seniors Appeal: ☆

Quiet/Active/Busy: Active to Busy
Nearby Attractions: Very short walk
to uptown attractions
Price Range: economy to moderate
Comments: Well maintained motel is
very convenient to uptown.

Good Nite Motel

S2275 US 12, Baraboo
608-356-4129
Area: Exit 92, Highway 12 close to Dells
on Baraboo side of Interstate
Swimming: Outdoor pool
Water Recreation Area: No
Kiddie Pool: No
Play Area: No
Picnic Area: No
Corridors: Exterior
Author's Rating: 1/2
Kid Appeal: ☆
Couples Appeal: ☆
Seniors Appeal: ☆
Quiet/Active/Busy: Quiet
Nearby Attractions: Shorter drive than
most to Ho-Chunk Casino
Price Range: economy to inexpensive
Comments: Low-cost place to stay,
slightly removed from immediate Dells/
Lake Delton area.

Grand Marquis

Highway 12, Lake Delton
608-254-4843
Area: Exit 92
Swimming: Indoor and outdoor pool
Water Recreation Area: Basic, a couple
of slides, but with some nice touches
Kiddie Pool: Yes
Play Area: Yes
Picnic Area: Yes
Corridors: Interior
Author's Rating: ☆☆1/2
Kid Appeal: ☆☆1/2
Couples Appeal: ☆☆1/2
Seniors Appeal: ☆☆1/2

Quiet/Active/Busy: Active
Nearby Attractions: Golf
Price Range: moderate to expensive
Comments: Excellent choice for couples
and seniors.

Heidi's Hideaway Resort

715 Canyon Road
608-253-4092
Area: East Shore of Lake Delton
Swimming: Outdoor pool
Water Recreation Area: No
Kiddie Pool: No
Play Area: Yes
Picnic Area: Yes
Corridors: Exterior, cabin style
Author's Rating: 1/2
Kid Appeal: ☆
Couples Appeal: ☆
Seniors Appeal: ☆
Quiet/Active/Busy: Quiet
Nearby Attractions: On premises
beach, drive to Parkway attractions
Price Range: economy to inexpensive
Comments: No frills lodging on water-
front.

Hiawatha Drive Resort

Hiawatha Drive
608-254-6551
Area: West Shore of Lake Delton
Swimming: waterfront
Water Recreation Area: No
Kiddie Pool: No
Play Area: No
Picnic Area: Yes
Corridors: Exterior
Author's Rating: ☆
Kid Appeal: ☆
Couples Appeal: ☆
Seniors Appeal: ☆
Quiet/Active/Busy: Quiet
Nearby Attractions: Drive to all
attractions
Price Range: economy to moderate
Comments: Not much to distinguish
from other waterfront choices.

Hilltop Motel

1100 Wisconsin Dells Parkway
608-253-3883
Area: Dells Parkway
Swimming: Outdoor pool
Water Recreation Area: No
Kiddie Pool: Yes
Play Area: Yes
Picnic Area: Yes
Corridors: Exterior
Author's Rating: ☆1/2
Kid Appeal: ☆1/2
Couples Appeal: ☆☆
Seniors Appeal: ☆1/2
Quiet/Active/Busy: Active
Nearby Attractions: Fairly convenient
to Noah's Ark and convenient to many
Parkway attractions
Price Range: economy to moderate
Comments: Economical choice that's
convenient to Noah's Ark.

Ho-Chunk Lodge

131 Canyon Road
608-254-2584
Area: Canyon Road on shore
of Lake Delton
Swimming: Outdoor pool
Water Recreation Area: Yes,
small pool with nifty waterslide
Kiddie Pool: No
Play Area: No
Picnic Area: Yes
Corridors: Condominium style
Author's Rating: ☆☆
Kid Appeal: ☆☆
Couples Appeal: ☆☆1/2
Seniors Appeal: ☆☆1/2
Quiet/Active/Busy: Quiet to Active
Nearby Attractions: Short drive to
Highway 12 and Parkway attractions
Price Range: moderate to luxury
Comments: Relatively small, convenient
waterfront location.

Holiday Inn and Aqua Dome
Exit 87 Off I-90
800-HOLIDAY
Area: Exit 87 Area
Swimming: Indoor and Outdoor pool
Water Recreation Area: Yes, indoor
and outdoor, both nice
Kiddie Pool: Indoor and Outdoor
Play Area: No
Picnic Area: No
Corridors: Interior
Author's Rating: ☆☆☆
Kid Appeal: ☆☆☆
Couples Appeal: ☆☆☆
Seniors Appeal: ☆☆☆
Quiet/Active/Busy: Active to Busy
Nearby Attractions: Short drive to
mini-golf and uptown, near Trapper's
Turn Golf Course
Price Range: moderate to expensive
Comments: Good water recreation areas,
located near fast-food restaurants in exit
87 area.

Holiday Motel
462 Wisconsin Dells Parkway
608-253-4751
Area: Exit 92 Area, Lake Delton
Swimming: Outdoor pool
Water Recreation Area: No
Kiddie Pool: No
Play Area: Yes
Picnic Area: Yes, with grills
Corridors: Exterior
Author's Rating: ☆1/2
Kid Appeal: ☆
Couples Appeal: ☆
Seniors Appeal: ☆
Quiet/Active/Busy: Active
Nearby Attractions: Short drive to
many Dells Parkway attractions
Price Range: economy to moderate
Comments: This older motel has a cer-
tain charm to it. A new sundeck was
added a few years ago.

Holiday Shores Campground and Resort
3900 River Road
608-254-2717
Area: River Road North
Swimming: Outdoor pool
Water Recreation Area: No
Kiddie Pool: No
Play Area: Yes
Picnic Area: Yes
Corridors: Campground
Author's Rating: ☆☆
Kid Appeal: ☆☆
Couples Appeal: ☆☆
Seniors Appeal: ☆☆
Quiet/Active/Busy: Active
Nearby Attractions: Approximately
four-mile drive to major attractions
Price Range: inexpensive to moderate
Comments: On Upper Dells waterfront,
with several waterfront activities avail-
able.

Indian Trail Motel
1013 Broadway
608-253-2641
Area: Exit 92 Area
Swimming: Indoor and outdoor pool
Water Recreation Area: No
Kiddie Pool: No
Play Area: Yes
Picnic Area: Yes
Corridors: Exterior
Author's Rating: ☆1/2
Kid Appeal: ☆
Couples Appeal: ☆☆
Seniors Appeal: ☆☆
Quiet/Active/Busy: Quiet to Active
Nearby Attractions: Six blocks
from uptown
Price Range: economy to moderate
Comments: Spacious grounds and
nearby restaurant make this a pleasant
place to stay.

Kalahari Resort and Conference Center

Under construction at time
of publication
Area: Exit 92, Highway 12 at I-90/94
Swimming: Outdoor pool
Water Recreation Area:
Yes—indoor and outdoor
Kiddie Pool: Yes
Price Range: expected to be luxury
Comments: This hotel is expected to be
another entry in the luxury market.

Kilbourn Inn Motel

813 Elm Street
608-254-4541
Swimming: No
Water Recreation Area: No
Kiddie Pool: No
Play Area: No
Picnic Area: No
Corridors: Exterior
Author's Rating: ☆
Kid Appeal: ☆
Couples Appeal: ☆
Seniors Appeal: ☆
Quiet/Active/Busy: Active to Busy
Nearby Attractions: Very short walk to
all uptown attractions and restaurants
Price Range: economy to moderate
Comments: Proximity to uptown attrac-
tions makes this small motel a good
economy choice.

King's Inn Motel

Mail: PO Box 497
Located just off Highway 12,
Lake Delton
Area: Near intersection of 12 and 23
Swimming: Indoor pool
Water Recreation Area: No
Kiddie Pool: No
Play Area: Yes
Picnic Area: Yes
Corridors: Exterior

Author's Rating: ☆
Kid Appeal: ☆
Couples Appeal: ☆
Seniors Appeal: ☆
Quiet/Active/Busy: Active
Nearby Attractions: Just a few blocks
from south-end Parkway attractions
such as Tommy Bartlett
Price Range: inexpensive to moderate
Comments: A little off by itself, but there
are several good restaurants within easy
walking distance.

Lake Aire Motel

436 Wisconsin Dells Parkway
608-253-5351
Area: south end of the Parkway
Swimming: Outdoor pool
Water Recreation Area: No
Kiddie Pool: No
Play Area: Yes
Picnic Area: Yes
Corridors: Exterior
Author's Rating: 1/2
Kid Appeal: ☆
Couples Appeal: 1/2
Seniors Appeal: 1/2
Quiet/Active/Busy: Quiet to Active
Nearby Attractions: Can't get much
closer to Tommy Bartlett attractions
Price Range: economy to inexpensive
Comments: South end Parkway location
is great, but better lodging choices are
available for economy travelers.

Lake Delton Motel

630 Wisconsin Dell Parkway South
(Highway 12)
608-254-2236
Area: Exit 92 Highway 12
Swimming: Outdoor pool
Water Recreation Area: No
Kiddie Pool: No
Play Area: Yes
Picnic Area: Yes

Corridors: Exterior
Author's Rating: ☆1/2
Kid Appeal: ☆
Couples Appeal: ☆
Seniors Appeal: ☆1/2
Quiet/Active/Busy: Quiet to Active
Nearby Attractions: Short drive or
long walk to Parkway attractions
Price Range: economy to moderate
Comments: Neatly maintained.

Lakeside Motel

210 Wisconsin Dells Parkway
608-253-2282
Area: on waterfront south end
of Dells Parkway
Swimming: Outdoor pool
Water Recreation Area: No
Kiddie Pool: No
Play Area: Yes
Picnic Area: Yes
Corridors: Exterior
Author's Rating: 1/2
Kid Appeal: ☆
Couples Appeal: 1/2
Seniors Appeal: 1/2
Quiet/Active/Busy: Quiet to Active
Nearby Attractions: South end
Dells Parkway attractions
Price Range: economy to expensive
Comments: Some small cottages available, free rowboats and paddleboats.

Lighthouse Cove
Condominium Resort

530 E Hiawatha Drive
800-790-2683
Area: Hiawatha
Swimming: Outdoor and indoor
Water Recreation Area: No
Kiddie Pool: No
Play Area: Yes
Picnic Area: Yes
Corridors: Condo-style

Author's Rating: ☆☆☆
Kid Appeal: ☆☆
Couples Appeal: ☆☆☆
Seniors Appeal: ☆☆☆
Quiet/Active/Busy: Quiet to Active
Price Range: expensive to luxury
Nearby Attractions: Drive to
all attractions
Comments: Condominiums on waterfront, very well done.

Luna Inn & Suites

1111 Wisconsin Dells Parkway
608-253-2661
Area: Dells Parkway
Swimming: Indoor and outdoor pool
Water Recreation Area: No
Kiddie Pool: No
Play Area: Yes, near picnic area
Picnic Area: Yes, nice in wooded area
Corridors: Exterior
Author's Rating: ☆1/2
Kid Appeal: ☆1/2
Couples Appeal: ☆☆
Seniors Appeal: ☆☆
Quiet/Active/Busy: Active to Busy
Nearby Attractions: Across the
Parkway from Noah's Ark
Price Range: inexpensive to expensive
Comments: Well maintained, located at
a convenient and bustling spot on the
Parkway.

Lynn-Dells Motel

N1405 Highway 12 & 16
Lyndon Station, Wisconsin 53944
608-254-2121
Area: Remote
Price Range: economy
Comments: This motel is noted here for
economy travelers. No pool, distant
location.

Lingen's Sandy Beach Resort

55 Dam Road
608-254-8533
Swimming: Outdoor pool
Water Recreation Area: No,
lakefront location
Kiddie Pool: No
Play Area: Yes
Picnic Area: Yes
Corridors: Exterior
Author's Rating: ☆
Kid Appeal: ☆
Couples Appeal: ☆
Seniors Appeal: ☆
Quiet/Active/Busy: Quiet
Nearby Attractions: Drive to
all attractions
Price Range: inexpensive to moderate
Comments: Rustic place on waterfront.

Malibu Inn

E10476 Highway 23
608-254-7102
Area: Exit 89 Area (Munroe Street)
Swimming: Outdoor pool
Water Recreation Area: No
Kiddie Pool: Yes
Play Area: Yes
Picnic Area: Yes
Corridors: Exterior
Author's Rating: ☆
Kid Appeal: ☆
Couples Appeal: ☆
Seniors Appeal: ☆
Quiet/Active/Busy: Quiet to Active
Nearby Attractions: Crystal Grand
Music Theater
Price Range: economy to inexpensive
Comments: A little off the main traffic
pattern, drive required to most attractions.

Mayflower Motel I and II

910 Wisconsin Dells Parkway
608-253-6471
Area: Dells Parkway
Swimming: Indoor and Outdoor pool
Water Recreation Area: No
Kiddie Pool: Yes
Play Area: Yes
Picnic Area: Yes
Corridors: Mostly Exterior
Author's Rating: ☆☆
Kid Appeal: ☆☆
Couples Appeal: ☆☆
Seniors Appeal: ☆☆
Quiet/Active/Busy: Active to Busy
Nearby Attractions: Situated between
Noah's Ark and Tommy Bartlett on
the Parkway
Price Range: inexpensive to expensive
Comments: Nice location with a wide
choice of rooms and suites, combines
two motels into one complex.

Monaco Motel

1310 Wisconsin Dells Parkway
608-254-7550
Area: Dells Parkway
Swimming: Indoor and Outdoor pool
Water Recreation Area: No
Kiddie Pool: Yes
Play Area: Yes
Picnic Area: Yes
Corridors: Exterior
Author's Rating: ☆☆
Kid Appeal: ☆☆
Couples Appeal: ☆1/2
Seniors Appeal: ☆☆
Quiet/Active/Busy: Active
Nearby Attractions: Noah's Ark
very convenient
Price Range: inexpensive to expensive
Comments: Some nice touches include
pleasant landscaping and an outdoor
pool with good kid appeal.

Monte Carlo Motel & Suites
350 E Hiawatha Dr
608-252-8761
Area: On west bank of Lake Delton
off the Parkway
Swimming: Outdoor pool
Water Recreation Area: No
Kiddie Pool: No
Play Area: Yes
Picnic Area: Yes
Corridors: Exterior
Author's Rating: ☆1/2
Kid Appeal: ☆
Couples Appeal: ☆☆
Seniors Appeal: ☆☆
Quiet/Active/Busy: Quiet
Nearby Attractions: Short drive or
long walk to Noah's Ark and
Tommy Bartlett
Price Range: inexpensive to expensive
Comments: A bit rustic, large grounds
and tranquil view of water, beach access
and dock.

Motel 6
Highway 12, turn left off I-90
at exit 92
608-254-5000
Area: Exit 92, Highway 12
toward Baraboo
Swimming: Outdoor pool
Water Recreation Area: No
Kiddie Pool: No
Play Area: No
Picnic Area: No
Corridors: Interior
Author's Rating: ☆1/2
Kid Appeal: ☆
Couples Appeal: ☆1/2
Seniors Appeal: ☆1/2
Quiet/Active/Busy: Quiet to Active
Nearby Attractions: Short drive
to all attractions
Price Range: inexpensive to moderate
Comments: Well-known budget chain
location opened in 1997.

Meadowbrook Resort
1533 River Road
608-253-3201
Area: River Road, a short drive
from uptown
Swimming: Outdoor pool
Water Recreation Area: Outdoor, cute
woodsy theme especially attractive to
younger kids
Kiddie Pool: Yes
Play Area: Yes
Picnic Area: Yes
Corridors: Many Exterior
Author's Rating: ☆☆1/2
Kid Appeal: ☆☆
Couples Appeal: ☆☆1/2
Seniors Appeal: ☆☆1/2
Quiet/Active/Busy: Quiet
Nearby Attractions: Short, pleasant
drive on River Road to uptown
Price Range: inexpensive to luxury
Comments: Hotel and cabins available,
great choice if you want some conve-
nience in a wooded setting.

New Concord Inn
411 Wisconsin Dells Parkway
608-254-4338
Area: Dells Parkway
Swimming: Indoor and Outdoor pool
Water Recreation Area: No
Kiddie Pool: Yes
Play Area: Yes
Picnic Area: Yes
Corridors: Interior
Author's Rating: ☆☆
Kid Appeal: ☆1/2
Couples Appeal: ☆☆
Seniors Appeal: ☆☆1/2
Quiet/Active/Busy: Active
Nearby Attractions: Tommy Bartlett
Price Range: inexpensive to expensive
Comments: Nothing spectacular in the
way of features, but very nicely done
with good appeal to adults and couples.

Old Newport Resort
S1156 Highway A
608-254-2029
Swimming: Outdoor pool
Water Recreation Area: No
Kiddie Pool: No
Play Area: Yes
Picnic Area: Yes
Corridors: Exterior, cottage style
Author's Rating: ☆
Kid Appeal: ☆
Couples Appeal: ☆
Seniors Appeal: ☆
Quiet/Active/Busy: Quiet
Nearby Attractions: Drive to
all attractions
Price Range: inexpensive to moderate
Comments: Rustic cottage-like accom-
modations.

Olympia Motel
207 Munroe, Highway 23
608-254-2800
Area: Munroe
Swimming: Indoor pool
Water Recreation Area: No
Kiddie Pool: No
Play Area: No
Picnic Area: No
Corridors: Exterior
Author's Rating: ☆
Kid Appeal: 1/2
Couples Appeal: ☆
Seniors Appeal: ☆
Quiet/Active/Busy: Quiet to Active
Nearby Attractions: Crystal Grand
Music Theater
Price Range: inexpensive to moderate
Comments: Munroe location requires
drive to attractions.

Paradise Motel
1700 Wisconsin Dells Parkway
608-254-7333
Area: Dells Parkway

Swimming: Outdoor pool
Water Recreation Area: No
Kiddie Pool: Yes
Play Area: Yes
Picnic Area: Yes
Corridors: Exterior
Author's Rating: ☆☆
Kid Appeal: ☆☆
Couples Appeal: ☆☆
Seniors Appeal: ☆☆
Quiet/Active/Busy: Active
Nearby Attractions: Extreme World
and other Parkway attractions
Price Range: economy to expensive
Comments: Nicely kept pool area, good
basic motel with higher-end prices for
suites.

Parkway Motel
223 Wisconsin Ave
608-254-7505
Area: Uptown
Swimming: No
Play Area: No
Picnic Area: Yes, small
Corridors: Mostly exterior
Author's Appeal: ☆
Kid Appeal: ☆
Couples Appeal: ☆
Seniors Appeal: ☆
Quiet/Active/Busy: Active
Nearby Attractions: Uptown
attractions are one block walk.
Price Range: economy to moderate
Comments: Very close to uptown, but
not a lot of amenities.

Parkview Motel
371 Park Drive
608-254-8182
Area: Off Hiawatha
a few blocks off the Parkway
Swimming: No
Water Recreation Area: No
Kiddie Pool: No

Play Area: Yes
Picnic Area: Yes
Corridors: Exterior
Author's Rating: 1/2
Kid Appeal: 1/2
Couples Appeal: 1/2
Seniors Appeal: 1/2
Quiet/Active/Busy: Quiet
Nearby Attractions: Short drive or fairly long walk to Parkway attractions
Price Range: inexpensive to moderate
Comments: Short walk to beach but better lodging choices in same price range are easy to find.

Pine Aire Motel & Suites
511 Wisconsin Dells Parkway
800-635-8627
Area: Dells Parkway
Swimming: Indoor pool
Water Recreation Area: No
Kiddie Pool: No
Play Area: Yes, with good, up-close view of a cemetery
Picnic Area: Yes
Corridors: Some interior
Author's Rating: ☆1/2
Kid Appeal: ☆
Couples Appeal: ☆☆
Seniors Appeal: ☆☆
Quiet/Active/Busy: Active
Nearby Attractions: Across the Parkway from Tommy Bartlett and other Park-way attractions
Price Range: economy to expensive
Comments: Range of choices from economy rooms to suites, and fairly convenient Parkway location.

Pine Beach Resort
481 Highway A
608-253-6361
Area: East shore of Lake Delton
Swimming: Outdoor pool and beach
Kiddie Pool: No

Play Area: Yes
Picnic Area: Yes
Corridors: Exterior
Author's Rating: 1/2
Kid Appeal: ☆
Couples Appeal: ☆
Seniors Appeal: ☆
Quiet/Active/Busy: Quiet
Nearby Attractions: Short drive to Parkway and uptown. Dock on premises and rowboats available.
Price Range: moderate to expensive
Comments: Quiet, rustic location.

Pine Dell Motel
1221 Wisconsin Dells Parkway
608-254-7660
Area: Wisconsin Dells Parkway
Swimming: Indoor and Outdoor pool
Water Recreation Area: No
Kiddie Pool: No
Play Area: Yes
Picnic Area: Yes
Corridors: Exterior
Author's Rating: ☆1/2
Kid Appeal: ☆
Couples Appeal: ☆1/2
Seniors Appeal: ☆1/2
Quiet/Active/Busy: Active
Nearby Attractions: Noah's Ark and other Parkway attractions
Price Range: inexpensive to expensive
Comments: Nothing spectacular but suitable lodging with fairly convenient Parkway location.

Playday Motel
1781 Wisconsin Dells Parkway
608-253-3961
Area: Dells Parkway
Swimming: Indoor and Outdoor pool
Water Recreation Area: No
Kiddie Pool: Yes
Play Area: Yes
Picnic Area: Yes

Corridors: Exterior
Author's Rating: ☆1/2
Kid Appeal: ☆☆
Couples Appeal: ☆1/2
Seniors Appeal: ☆1/2
Quiet/Active/Busy: Active
Nearby Attractions: Adjacent to
Family Land, near Crazy King
Ludwig's
Price Range: economy to moderate
Comments: Great, though busy, location
convenient to Family Land and Parkway
attractions in the area.

Pleasant View Motel

1621 Wisconsin Dells Parkway
608-254-8180
Area: Dells Parkway
Swimming: Indoor and Outdoor pool
Water Recreation Area: No
Kiddie Pool: No
Play Area: Yes
Picnic Area: Yes
Corridors: Exterior
Author's Rating: ☆1/2
Kid Appeal: ☆
Couples Appeal: ☆☆1/2
Seniors Appeal: ☆☆1/2
Quiet/Active/Busy: Active to Busy
Nearby Attractions: Family Land
Price Range: inexpensive to expensive
Comments: Nothing extraordinary, but
nicely done.

Polynesian Resort

Highway 13 just off I-90
608-254-2883
Area: Exit 87
Swimming: Indoor and Outdoor pool
Water Recreation Area: Indoor and
Outdoor, among the very best in
the Dells
Kiddie Pool: Yes
Play Area: Yes, quite nice
Picnic Area: Yes

Corridors: Interior
Author's Rating: ☆☆☆
Kid Appeal: ☆☆☆
Couples Appeal: ☆☆☆
Seniors Appeal: ☆☆☆
Quiet/Active/Busy: Active to Busy
Nearby Attractions: Trapper's Turn
Golf Course, short drive to other
attractions
Price Range: expensive to luxury
Comments: One of the most spectacular
hotels in the Dells, with a wonderful out-
door water area. We think the Polynesian
carries out its theme better than any hotel
in the area.

Rain-bow Motel

612 Vine Street
608-254-7606
Area: Just off Broadway
Swimming: Outdoor pool
Water Recreation Area: No
Kiddie Pool: No
Play Area: Yes
Picnic Area: Yes
Corridors: Exterior
Author's Rating: ☆
Kid Appeal: ☆
Couples Appeal: ☆
Seniors Appeal: ☆
Quiet/Active/Busy: Quiet to Active
Nearby Attractions: Fairly short walk
to uptown attractions
Price Range: economy to moderate
Comments: A low-cost place to stay,
located fairly close to uptown.

Raintree Resort

1435 Wisconsin Dells Parkway
608-253-4FUN
Area: Dells Parkway
Swimming: Indoor and Outdoor pool
Water Recreation Area: Yes, indoor
very nice, outdoor not as great but
above average

Kiddie Pool: Yes
Play Area: No
Picnic Area: Yes
Corridors: Interior
Author's Rating: ☆☆☆
Kid Appeal: ☆☆☆
Couples Appeal: ☆☆☆
Seniors Appeal: ☆☆☆
Quiet/Active/Busy: Active to Busy
Nearby Attractions: Short walk
to Noah's Ark and other Parkway
attractions
Price Range: expensive to luxury
Comments: A bit pricey, but one of the
top places to stay in the Dells. Our pick
for best overall hotel on the Parkway.

Ramada Limited

1073 Wisconsin Dells Parkway South
(Highway 12)
608-254-2218
Area: Exit 92
Swimming: Indoor pool
Water Recreation Area: No
Kiddie Pool: No
Play Area: No
Picnic Area: No
Corridors: Interior
Author's Rating: ☆
Kid Appeal: ☆
Couples Appeal: ☆1/2
Seniors Appeal: ☆☆
Quiet/Active/Busy: Quiet to Active
Nearby Attractions: Fairly short drive
to major attractions
Price Range: moderate to expensive
Comments: Basic accommodations
away from the Parkway hubub.

River Bay Motel

1024 River Road
608-254-6114
Area: River Road, a few blocks
from uptown

Swimming: Outdoor pool
Water Recreation Area: No
Kiddie Pool: No
Play Area: Yes
Picnic Area: Yes
Corridors: Exterior
Author's Rating: ☆
Kid Appeal: ☆
Couples Appeal: ☆
Seniors Appeal: ☆
Quiet/Active/Busy: Quiet to Active
Nearby Attractions: Short walk to
uptown attractions
Price Range: economy to inexpensive
Comments: Modest, low-cost lodging,
extremely convenient to uptown.

River Inn

1015 River Road
608-253-1231
Area: River Road a few blocks
from uptown
Swimming: Outdoor and indoor pool
Water Recreation Area: No
Kiddie Pool: No
Play Area: Yes, across the street
from hotel
Picnic Area: No
Corridors: Interior
Author's Rating: ☆☆
Kid Appeal: ☆
Couples Appeal: ☆☆1/2
Seniors Appeal: ☆☆1/2
Quiet/Active/Busy: Quiet to Active
Nearby Attractions: Short walk to
uptown attractions
Price Range: moderate to expensive
Comments: Great river views from some
rooms, adult atmosphere, in-house
restaurant, and location make it good
choice for adults who want convenience
to uptown.

Rivers Edge Resort & Motel

S1196 Highway A
608-254-7707
Area: East shore off Lake Delton
on Lower Dells
Swimming: Outdoor pool
Water Recreation Area: No
Kiddie Pool: No
Play Area: Yes
Picnic Area: Yes
Corridors: Exterior, log cabin style motel
Author's Rating: ☆☆
Kid Appeal: ☆1/2
Couples Appeal: ☆☆
Seniors Appeal: ☆☆
Quiet/Active/Busy: Quiet to Active
Nearby Attractions: Short drive to
Highway 12 and Parkway attractions
Price Range: inexpensive to expensive
Comments: Has suites up to three bed-
rooms, fireplaces, beach, and boat
access.

Riviera Motel

811 Wisconsin Dells Parkway
608-253-1051
Area: Wisconsin Dells Parkway
Swimming: Indoor and Outdoor pool
Water Recreation Area: No
Kiddie Pool: No
Play Area: No
Picnic Area: No
Corridors: Exterior
Author's Rating: ☆1/2
Kid Appeal: ☆
Couples Appeal: ☆☆
Seniors Appeal: ☆☆
Quiet/Active/Busy: Active to Busy
Nearby Attractions: Across Dells
Parkway midway between Tommy
Bartlett and Noah's Ark
Price Range: inexpensive to expensive
Comments: Convenient Parkway loca-
tion, also near several table-service
restaurants.

Robin Hood Resort

670 E Lake Ave
608-254-7007
Area: Hiawatha Drive
Swimming: Outdoor pool
Water Recreation Area: No
Kiddie Pool: No
Play Area: Yes
Picnic Area: Yes
Corridors: Exterior
Author's Rating: 1/2
Kid Appeal: ☆
Couples Appeal: ☆
Seniors Appeal: ☆
Quiet/Active/Busy: Quiet
Nearby Attractions: Drive to attractions
Price Range: economy to moderate
Comments: One of a number of similar
waterfront places on Hiawatha Drive.

Rodeway Inn

350 W Munroe Street
888-888-6050
Area: Munroe, Exit 89
Swimming: Indoor pool
Water Recreation Area: No
Kiddie Pool: No
Play Area: No
Picnic Area: No
Corridors: interior
Author's Rating: ☆1/2
Kid Appeal: ☆1/2
Couples Appeal: ☆☆
Seniors Appeal: ☆☆
Quiet/Active/Busy: Quiet to Active
Nearby Attractions: Convenient to
Crystal Grand Music Theater
Price Range: inexpensive to moderate
Comments: Newest motel in Munroe
Street area located next to the Crystal
Grand.

Mr. B's Sahara Motel

E10375 Highway 23
608-254-2505 or 800-822-7768
Area: Munroe Street
Swimming: No
Water Recreation Area: No
Kiddie Pool: No
Play Area: No
Picnic Area: No
Corridors: Exterior
Author's Rating: 1/2
Kid Appeal: ☆
Couples Appeal: ☆
Seniors Appeal: ☆
Quiet/Active/Busy: Quiet to Active
Nearby Attractions: Crystal Grand
Music Theater
Price Range: economy to inexpensive
Comments: No-frills motel with little
atmosphere.

Sand County Service Company

PO Box 409, Lake Delton 53940
Office located on Munroe Street
608-254-6551
Manages and rents private cottages,
condos and vacation homes. Many
choices, most with access to pools,
beaches and other amenities

Sandman Inn

651 Wisconsin Dells Parkway
608-253-1811
Area: Dells Parkway
Swimming: Outdoor pool
Water Recreation Area: No
Kiddie Pool: No
Play Area: Yes, small
Picnic Area: Yes, small
Corridors: Exterior
Author's Rating: 1/2
Kid Appeal: ☆
Couples Appeal: ☆
Seniors Appeal: ☆

Quiet/Active/Busy: Active to Busy
Nearby Attractions: Across Dells
Parkway midway between Tommy
Bartlett and Noah's Ark
Price Range: economy to moderate
Comments: Economy with fairly conve-
nient location on the Parkway.

Sands Motel

124 Wisconsin Dells Parkway South
(Highway 12)
608-254-7447
Area: Exit 92 toward town
Swimming: Outdoor pool
Water Recreation Area: No
Kiddie Pool: No
Play Area: Yes
Picnic Area: Yes
Corridors: Exterior
Author's Rating: 1/2
Kid Appeal: ☆
Couples Appeal: ☆
Seniors Appeal: ☆
Quiet/Active/Busy: Active
Nearby Attractions: Reasonable walk
to Tommy Bartlett attractions
Price Range: economy to moderate
Comments: Economy located off the
Parkway.

Shady Lawn Motel

1038 River Road
608-254-2211
Area: Dells Parkway
Swimming: Outdoor pool
Water Recreation Area: No
Kiddie Pool: No
Play Area: Yes
Picnic Area: Yes
Corridors: Exterior
Author's Rating: ☆
Kid Appeal: ☆
Couples Appeal: ☆
Seniors Appeal: ☆

Quiet/Active/Busy: Quiet
Nearby Attractions: Short walk
to uptown attractions
Price Range: economy to moderate
Comments: Modest, low-cost place to
stay near uptown.

Shady Nook Motel
Highway 12-16 just north
of Wisconsin Dells
Area: Just north of town
Swimming: Outdoor pool
Water Recreation Area: No
Kiddie Pool: No
Play Area: Yes
Picnic Area: Yes
Corridors: Exterior
Author's Rating: 1/2
Kid Appeal: ☆
Couples Appeal: 1/2
Seniors Appeal: ☆
Quiet/Active/Busy: Quiet to Active
Nearby Attractions: Very short drive
or walk across highway to mini-golf,
short drive uptown, Trappers Turn
golf course nearby
Price Range: economy to moderate
Comments: There are better choices in
this price range.

Shamrock Motel
1321 Wisconsin Dells Parkway
608-254-8054
Area: Dells Parkway
Swimming: Indoor and Outdoor pool
Water Recreation Area: Nice touches
to pools, but not a true water park
Kiddie Pool: Yes
Play Area: Yes, nice
Picnic Area: Yes, outdoor grills
Corridors: Exterior
Author's Rating: ☆1/2
Kid Appeal: ☆1/2
Couples Appeal: ☆1/2
Seniors Appeal: *☆1/2

Quiet/Active/Busy: Active to Busy
Nearby Attractions: Across Dells
Parkway near Noah's Ark
Price Range: inexpensive to moderate
Comments: Nothing spectacular but
good value, solid place on the Parkway.

Skyline Hotel and Suites
1970 Wisconsin Dells Parkway
608-253-4841
Area: Dells Parkway
Swimming: Indoor and Outdoor pool
Water Recreation Area:
"indoor sea serpent" slide
Kiddie Pool: Yes
Play Area: Yes
Picnic Area: Yes
Corridors: Exterior and Interior
Author's Rating: ☆☆1/2
Kid Appeal: ☆☆1/2
Couples Appeal: ☆☆1/2
Seniors Appeal: ☆☆1/2
Quiet/Active/Busy: Active to Busy
Nearby Attractions: Ducks, Big Chief
and other Dells Parkway attractions
Price Range: moderate to luxury
Comments: Solid if not spectacular, and
convenient to many attractions.

Southern Comfort Motel
N530 Highway 12
608-253-4193
Area: About 2 miles from Dells
on Highway 12
Swimming: Outdoor
Water Recreation Area: No
Kiddie Pool: No
Play Area: Yes
Picnic Area: Yes
Corridors: Exterior
Author's Rating: ☆
Kid Appeal: ☆
Couples Appeal: ☆
Seniors Appeal: ☆
Quiet/Active/Busy: Quiet

Price Range: economy to moderate
Nearby Attractions: Drive to
all attractions
Comments: Pretty far off the beaten
track, but peaceful.

Spring Brook
420 Birchwood Road
608-254-4349
Area: Just west of I-90/94
Swimming: Outdoor pool
Play Area: Yes
Picnic Area: Yes
Corridors: Exterior (vacation homes)
Author's Rating: ☆☆
Kid Appeal: ☆
Couples Appeal: ☆☆
Seniors Appeal: ☆☆
Quiet/Active/Busy: Quiet
Price Range: moderate to luxury
Nearby Attractions: Drive to
all attractions
Comments: Vacation homes for rent
located on a small lake near the Dells.

Spring Hill Motel
400 Vine Street
608-253-4121
Area: About 6 blocks from uptown,
a few blocks off Broadway
Swimming: Outdoor
Water Recreation Area: No
Kiddie Pool: No
Play Area: Yes
Picnic Area: Yes
Corridors: Exterior
Author's Rating: ☆
Kid Appeal: ☆
Couples Appeal: ☆
Seniors Appeal: ☆
Quiet/Active/Busy: Quiet
Price Range: economy to moderate
Nearby Attractions: Walk to
uptown attractions

Comments: Of the uptown-area
motels, one of the longer hikes to
uptown attractions.

Stanton Motel
931 N Capital Street
608-254-7361
Area: About a block off Broadway
and 3 blocks from uptown
Swimming: No
Water Recreation Area: No
Kiddie Pool: No
Play Area: No
Picnic Area: Yes
Corridors: Exterior
Author's Rating: 1/2
Kid Appeal: ☆
Couples Appeal: ☆
Seniors Appeal: ☆
Quiet/Active/Busy: Quiet to Active
Price Range: economy
Nearby Attractions: Walk to
uptown attractions
Comments: If you want economy with
no frills and an uptown location, this is
the place.

Star Motel Resort
1531-1571 Wisconsin Dells Parkway
608-254-2051
Area: Dells Parkway
Swimming: Indoor and Outdoor pools
Water Recreation Area: No
Kiddie Pool: Yes
Play Area: Yes
Picnic Area: Yes
Corridors: Exterior
Author's Rating: ☆☆
Kid Appeal: ☆☆
Couples Appeal: ☆☆
Seniors Appeal: ☆☆1/2
Quiet/Active/Busy: Active to Busy

Nearby Attractions: Across Dells
Parkway from Storybook Gardens,
cross the Parkway and walk to
Noah's Ark
Price Range: inexpensive to moderate
Comments: Combination of two motels,
restaurant on-site, large grounds in back.

Sunset Cove Condominiums
see Sand County Service Company
listing

Super 8 Motel
Exit 87, Highway 13
608-254-6464
Area: Exit 87
Swimming: Indoor pool
Water Recreation Area: No
Kiddie Pool: No
Play Area: No
Picnic Area: Yes, small
Corridors: Interior
Author's Rating: ☆1/2
Kid Appeal: ☆
Couples Appeal: ☆1/2
Seniors Appeal: ☆1/2
Quiet/Active/Busy: Active
Nearby Attractions: Near Trapper
Turn Golf Course
Price Range: economy to moderate
Comments: Economy at Exit 87, near
fast food, relatively new and nicely
maintained.

Surfside Motel
231 Wisconsin Dells Parkway South
608-254-7594
Area: Exit 92 toward town
Swimming: Outdoor pool
Water Recreation Area: No
Kiddie Pool: No
Play Area: No
Picnic Area: Yes, small
Corridors: Exterior

Author's Rating: ☆
Kid Appeal: ☆
Couples Appeal: ☆1/2
Seniors Appeal: ☆1/2
Quiet/Active/Busy: Quiet to Active
Nearby Attractions: Short drive to
Dells Parkway, walk to antique shops
and fast food/arcade
Price Range: economy to moderate
Comments: Convenient to an antique
mall. Ask to stay in newer building
located in rear.

Tamarack Condominium Resort
Managed by Sand County
Service Company
Area: Just west of exit 89 off I-90/94
Swimming: Indoor and outdoor pool
Kiddie Pool: Yes
Play Area: Yes
Picnic Area: Yes
Corridors: Exterior
Author's Rating: ☆☆1/2
Kid Appeal: ☆☆
Couples Appeal: ☆☆
Seniors Appeal: ☆☆
Quiet/Active/Busy: Quiet
Nearby Attractions: Short drive
to all attractions
Price Range: moderate to luxury
Comments: A little out of the way, but
quite pleasant.

Thunderbird Resort
1040 E Hiawatha Drive
608-253-5031
Area: West bank of Lake Delton
Swimming: Indoor pool
Water Recreation Area: No
Kiddie Pool: No
Play Area: Yes
Picnic Area: Yes
Corridors: Exterior
Author's Rating: ☆

Kid Appeal: ☆
Couples Appeal: ☆
Seniors Appeal: ☆
Quiet/Active/Busy: Quiet to Active
Nearby Attractions: Waterfront has beach and boat access, drive to Parkway attractions
Price Range: inexpensive to moderate
Comments: One of several modest but aequate places to stay on Hiawatha Drive.

Top Hat Motel
812 River Road
608-253-5431
Area: River Road just off Broadway
Swimming: None
Water Recreation Area: No
Kiddie Pool: No
Play Area: No
Picnic Area: No
Corridors: Exterior
Author's Rating: ☆1/2
Kid Appeal: 1/2
Couples Appeal: ☆1/2
Seniors Appeal: ☆1/2
Quiet/Active/Busy: Quiet to Busy
Nearby Attractions: Less than one block from uptown action
Price Range: economy to moderate
Comments: Another good choice for adults who want no-frills convenience to uptown attractions.

Travelodge
1113 Broadway
608-253-4271
Area: Broadway
Swimming: Outdoor pool
Water Recreation Area: No
Kiddie Pool: No
Play Area: Yes
Picnic Area: Yes
Corridors: Exterior

Author's Rating: ☆1/2
Kid Appeal: ☆
Couples Appeal: ☆
Seniors Appeal: ☆
Quiet/Active/Busy: Quiet to Active
Nearby Attractions: Moderate distance walk to uptown
Price Range: inexpensive to expensive
Comments: Nicely maintained, yet another option with adequate convenience to uptown.

Treasure Island Hotel & Suites
1701 Wisconsin Dells Parkway
608-254-8560
Area: Dells Parkway
Swimming: Indoor and Outdoor pool
Water Recreation Area: Yes, and if you guessed a pirate theme, you're right!
Kiddie Pool: Yes
Play Area: No
Picnic Area: No
Corridors: Interior
Author's Rating: ☆☆1/2
Kid Appeal: ☆☆☆
Couples Appeal: ☆☆☆
Seniors Appeal: ☆☆1/2
Quiet/Active/Busy: Busy
Nearby Attractions: Shares common parking lot with Family Land
Price Range: expensive to luxury
Comments: One of the newer hotels in the area, bustling atmosphere.

Twi-Lite Motel
111 Wisconsin Dells Parkway
608-253-1911
Area: Exit 92 toward town
Swimming: Outdoor pool
Water Recreation Area: No
Kiddie Pool: No
Play Area: Yes, small
Picnic Area: Yes, small
Corridors: Exterior

Author's Rating: 1/2
Kid Appeal: 1/2
Couples Appeal: ☆
Seniors Appeal: ☆
Quiet/Active/Busy: Active to Busy
Nearby Attractions: Short drive to
Parkway attractions, near antique
shops and fast food/arcade
Price Range: economy to moderate
Comments: Economy on the Parkway.

Villa Inn
711 Wisconsin Dells Parkway
608-254-2340
Area: Wisconsin Dells Parkway
Swimming: Outdoor pool
Water Recreation Area: No
Kiddie Pool: No
Play Area: Yes, small
Picnic Area: Yes, small
Corridors: Exterior
Author's Rating: 1/2
Kid Appeal: 1/2
Couples Appeal: ☆
Seniors Appeal: ☆
Quiet/Active/Busy: Active to Busy
Nearby Attractions: Across the
Parkway near Tommy Bartlett
and Noah's Ark
Price Range: economy to moderate
Comments: Economy on the Parkway.

Wilderness Hotel & Golf Resort
511 E Adams Street
(just off Highway 12)
608-253-9729
Area: Exit 92
Swimming: Indoor and Outdoor pool
Water Recreation Area: Yes, indoor
and outdoor are both among the best
in the Dells

Kiddie Pool: Yes
Play Area: Yes
Picnic Area: Yes
Corridors: Interior
Author's Rating: ☆☆☆
Kid Appeal: ☆☆☆
Couples Appeal: ☆☆☆
Seniors Appeal: ☆☆☆
Quiet/Active/Busy: Active
Nearby Attractions: Adjacent golf
course, short drive to Parkway
attractions
Price Range: expensive to luxury
Comments: One of the more spectacu-
lar hotels in the Dells area, with its
theme nicely carried out and excellent
water recreation areas.

Wintergreen Resort & Conference Center
Just off Highway 12 at I-90
608-254-2285
Area: Exit 92
Swimming: Indoor and Outdoor pools
Water Recreation Area: Indoor and
outdoor; very nice polar theme
Kiddie Pool: Yes
Play Area: Yes
Picnic Area: Yes
Corridors: Interior
Author's Rating: ☆☆☆
Kid Appeal: ☆☆☆
Couples Appeal: ☆☆☆
Seniors Appeal: ☆☆☆
Quiet/Active/Busy: Active to Busy
Nearby Attractions: Drive to all
major attractions
Price Range: expensive to luxury
Comments: An all-suite hotel, fast food
nearby plus on-site restaurant, one of the
Dells more spectacular hotels.

Campgrounds

American World
County A and Highway 12,
off the Parkway
Phone 608-253-4451
RV full hookups only; can share many
of the amenities of the American
World Resort including indoor/outdoor
pools, game room, and tennis.

Arrowhead Resort & Campground
Arrowhead Road
608-254-7344
Full range of campsites and hookups,
outdoor pool, and lots of activities

Baraboo Hills Campground
Terrytown Road, Baraboo
608-356-8505
Facilities include outdoor pool and
full hookups

Bass Lake Campground
Lyndon Station, WI
666-2311
Good distance north of Dells, water/
electric hookups and cabins available,
beach

Bonanza Campground and RV Resort
Wisconsin Dells
254-8124
Outdoor pool, mini-golf, wide range
of campsites and hookups

Dell Boo Campground
Wisconsin Dells
356-5898
Outdoor pool, hiking, wide range
of campsites and hookups

Dells Timberland Camping Resort
Wisconsin Dells
254-2429
Outdoor pool, mini-golf, wide range
of campsites and hookups

Devil's Lake State Park
Baraboo
356-8301
One of Wisconsin's most outstanding
and popular parks, beach, hiking,
some electric hookup sites

Eagle Flats Campground
Wisconsin Dells
254-2764
Outdoor pool, range of campsites
and hookups (no full hookups)

Erickson's Teepee Park Campground
Wisconsin Dells
253-3122
Outdoor pool, mini-golf, wide range
of campsites and hookups

Fox Hill RV Park
Baraboo
356-5890
Water and electric hookups, cabins,
outdoor pool

Holiday Shores Campground and Resort
Wisconsin Dells
254-2717
Range of hookups (no full hookups),
beach, cabins, outdoor pool, no
laundry

K&L Campground

Wisconsin Dells
586-4720
Range of hookups (no full hookups),
beach, outdoor pool, no laundry,
located on small lake just east of Dells

Lake of the Dells Campground

Wisconsin Dells
254-6485
Full range of campsites, hookups and
services, beach, cabins, outdoor pool

Mirror Lake State Park

Baraboo
254-2333
State park with some electric hookup
sites, showers, hiking, beach. Handicap
accessible fishing pier

Red Oak Campground

Baraboo
356-7304
Campsites, full hookups, outdoor pool

Rocky Arbor State Park

Small state park fairly conveniently
located to Dells attractions, limited
sites with electric hookup

Sherwood Forest Camping and RV Park

Wisconsin Dells
254-7080
Range of campsites and hookups,
outdoor pool, located just north of
Dells attractions

Southfork Campground and RV Park

Wisconsin Dells
253-2267
Wide range of campsites and hookups,
outdoor pool, about 12 blocks from
uptown Dells

Stand Rock Campground

Wisconsin Dells
253-2169
Range of hookups and campsites,
outdoor pool, north of Dells on
Stand Rock Road

Wisconsin Dells KOA

Wisconsin Dells
254-4177
Range of hookups and campsites,
outdoor pool, just north of Dells
on Stand Rock Road

Yogi Bear's Jellystone Park

Wisconsin Dells (Lake Delton)
254-2568
Range of hookups and campsites,
outdoor pool, south of Lake Delton

Yukon Trails Campground

Lyndon Station
666-3261
Range of hookups and campsites,
outdoor pool, no laundry

A Primer On Bed and Breakfasts

Bed-and-breakfast lodging isn't for everyone. Some people swear that they will stay in no other type of lodging, while others try a B&B and don't wish to repeat the experience. Generally, bed and breakfast lodging is often an enjoyable experience for couples and seniors, but families with children—especially younger children—frequently find that motels are a better choice. Most inns strive for a home-and-hearth feel and take pride in personalized service. Some travelers like this approach to lodging, but some prefer the atmosphere of a motel with a strictly-business desk clerk instead of a new-found friend in the form of the innkeeper.

If you want to try a bed-and-breakfast inn, be sure to take some time to discuss the accommodations in some detail. Room shapes and sizes are not uniform as they are in a motel, since inns are usually old homes that have been remodeled several times over the years. Be sure to ask a lot of questions. For example, in B&Bs, there is no universal meaning to a "double" room—it might be a room with one double bed, two double beds, or perhaps two twin beds. Also, there is no sure bet your room will have a private bath unless you specifically are told so.

If you are traveling with children, and want to experience an inn, make sure that you determine the inn's policy about the age of guests. Some inns have a formal minimum age. Other B&Bs allow children, but many of those seem to do so grudgingly. My experience suggests that for families, both innkeepers and children are usually happier if you choose a motel instead of a B&B. Pets are generally not allowed at most inns, but it doesn't hurt to ask.

Because they often contain valuable antique furnishings, many inns have a no-smoking policy, so it pays to ask about this if you're a smoker. Also, many B&Bs accept major credit cards, but enough of them don't accept plastic that it's worthwhile to ask when making your reservation. A final word of advice: because inns have only a few rooms, a no-show hurts the innkeeper's pocketbook much more than a no-show hurts a motel with 200 rooms. For this reason, inns typically require a longer cancellation period than that of a motel—many ask for several days notice for cancellations. You may forfeit your deposit (usually one night's cost) if you cancel after the deadline, so be sure to ask about the policy.

Bed-and-Breakfast Listing

Rates for Bed-and-Breakfast lodging in the Dells range from around $50 to $150 in season, depending on accommodations.

Bennett House

825 Oak Street
608-254-2500
One block to uptown, once the home of the famous Dells photographer (see page 62.)

Buckley House

3765 County Highway P
608-586-5752
A 15-20 minute drive from the Dells. Victorian home with comfortable living room. Holds Apple Butter Days in October, featuring making of apple butter on an open fire.

Calico House

240 S. Burritt Avenue
608-254-2400
South of the Parkway in Lake Delton. Convenient location and "home away from home" atmosphere.

Dells Carver Inn

1270 E. Hiawatha Drive
608-254-4766
Waterfront location on Lake Delton with beach. Original hand-carved, hand-painted Victorian Santas, Woodlyns, and Trolls crafted on-site.

Hawk's View

E11344 Pocahontas Circle
608-254-2979
Located on bluff overlooking river.

Pinehaven

E13083 Highway 33, Baraboo
608-356-3489
Convenient to Circus World and Devil's Lake Park.

Swallow's Nest

141 Sarrington
608-254-6900
Two blocks off Highway 12 in Lake Delton. English-style decorating in one of the newest B&Bs in the area.

Terrace Hill

922 River Road
608-253-9363
Less than two blocks from uptown. Victorian home located on small bluff overlooking River Road.

Thunder Valley Inn

W15344 Waubeek Road
608-254-4145
Scandinavian theme B&B and restaurant about two miles north of Dells, including chatauquas with authentic Scandinavian food and entertainment on summer evenings.

The White Rose

910 River Road
608-254-4724
Pleasant location near uptown area. Garden Café also serves other meals.

Our Favorites For Lodging

The following lists were compiled from a combination of our opinions and those of other visitors. All listings are in alphabetical order, *not* by any sort of ranking. For more information about the various lodging places, refer to the detailed alphabetical listing.

Our Favorite Lodging with Water Recreation Areas

Water recreation areas are the newest and hottest trend in Dells lodging. This has created some confusion for consumers, because some motels claim to have a "water recreation area" that's really just a glorified pool, while other water recreation areas are true mini-water parks with several slides.

Head and shoulders above the rest in the Dells are *Black Wolf Lodge*, the *Polynesian,* and the *Wilderness Hotel.* All three have spectacular outdoor and fine indoor areas. Black Wolf seems to be determined to set the indoor standard. Close behind those three are the *Wintergreen Resort, Copa Cabana, Raintree Resort, Treasure Island, Holiday Inn,* and *Chula Vista,* all of which have fine indoor and outdoor areas. Hotels with nice outdoor areas only include *Meadowbrook Resort, Caribbean Club,* and *Carousel Inn & Suites.* The *Atlantis* has a nice indoor area and their outdoor pool is nicely landscaped. Just open but not yet reviewed are *Camelot* and *Kalahari,* which promise to have spectacular indoor and outdoor areas.

Since this is a hotly competitive feature among lodging places, new facilities are being added quickly. If a water recreation area is high on your priorities list, review the motel's literature carefully and ask specifically about the number and length of water slides.

Our Lodging Favorites For Couples— Moderate to Luxury Cost

Alakai Hotel
Best Western Ambassador Inn
Black Wolf Lodge
Caribbean Club
Chula Vista
D'Amour's Big Cedar Lodge
Diamond Hotel
Lighthouse Cove Condominiums
Meadowbrook Resort
New Concord Inn
Polynesian Resort
Raintree
River Inn
Sand County Service Company
(condos and rentals)
Wilderness Hotel
Wintergreen Resort

Our Lodging Favorites For Couples— Economy to Moderate Cost

Cliffside Resort
Comfort Inn
Deer Trail Motel
Luna Inn
Pleasantview Motel
Riviera Motel
Star Motel
Top Hat Motel

Our Lodging Favorites For Seniors— Moderate to Luxury Cost

Alakai Hotel
Best Western Ambassador Inn
D'Amour's Big Cedar Lodge
Diamond Hotel
Grand Marquis
Meadowbrook Resort
New Concord Inn
River Inn

Sand County Service Company
(condos and rentals)
Wilderness Hotel
Wintergreen Resort

Our Lodging Favorites
For Seniors—
Economy to Moderate Cost
Cliffside Resort
Comfort Inn
Days Inn
Deer Trail Motel
Indian Trail Motel
Lake Delton Motel
Luna Inn
Pleasantview Motel
Ramada Ltd.
Riviera Motel
Skyline Hotel
Star Motel
Top Hat Motel

Our Lodging Favorites
For Families With Children—
Moderate to Luxury Cost
Atlantis Hotel
Black Wolf Lodge
Caribbean Club Resort
Chula Vista
Copa Cabana
Flamingo Motel
Holiday Inn Aqua Dome
Meadowbrook Resort
Polynesian Resort
Raintree
Treasure Island
Wilderness Hotel
Wintergreen Resort

Our Lodging Favorites
For Families With Children—
Economy to Moderate Cost
American World
Blackhawk Motel
Carousel Inn & Suites
Comfort Inn
Dells Eagle Motel
Hilltop Motel
Holiday Motel
Luna Inn
Mayflower Motel
Monaco Motel
Paradise Motel
Pine Dell Motel
Playday Motel
Shamrock Motel
Star Motel

Most Conveniently Located
Campgrounds
To Exit 92 Area:
Red Oak Campground
Yogi Bear's Jellystone Park
Dell Boo Campground

To Uptown Wisconsin Dells:
Southfork Campground
K&L Campground
Sherwood Forest Campground

To Wisconsin Dells Parkway:
American World Resort and RV Park
(RV only)
Bonanza Campground and RV Resort
Sherwood Forest Campground
Wisconsin Dells KOA
Rocky Arbor State Park

The Secrets of Truly Great Fudge

Have you ever wanted to be a star on Broadway? Skip all those dancing and singing lessons and learn how to make fudge. Every summer day and evening, thousands of people strolling down Broadway (the one in the Dells, not New York) stop to watch the fascinating art of fudge making. Multiply those thousands of daily onlookers by the number of summer days and a Broadway fudge-maker attracts an audience that the biggest New York theater star would envy.

While the process of fudge-making is interesting, it's the finished product that gets the most attention. Getting that tasty chocolate flavor and creamy texture are a lot more difficult than you might think. After a thorough procedure including observation, in-depth interviews, and (the best part of all) taste-tests, we have uncovered some of the secrets to making great fudge.

Skilled fudge-makers may appear casual in how they measure ingredients and keep track of the fudge-in-process, but that's because most have been practicing their art for years, making perhaps a dozen batches daily, for decades. But as casual as they appear, any fudge-making pro will tell you that a close eye on measurements and cooking temperatures are the first steps to fine fudge.

You may note that the fudge table has a thick marble top. Marble is the favorite tabletop material of the old-school fudge-makers because it draws the heat from the hot fudge mixture at just the right speed. It doesn't cool too quickly, allowing the fudge-maker plenty of time to finish the fudge. Some stores have installed stainless steel tables with controllable heating/cooling elements imbedded in the tabletop, but any veteran fudge-maker will tell you that marble is preferable, and the stainless steel tables should be relegated for lesser candies such as peanut brittle. The pros also claim that the dense marble also makes the table easy to clean between batches. Sadly, a number of Dells stores have switched to stainless steel. It's hard to stop the march of modern technology.

Mixing (called "beating" in the fudge world) requires not only strong arms, but skill as well. The marshmallow, fudge, and chocolate pieces (or other flavors, depending on the type of fudge being made) must be beat to just the right texture. Overbeating will result in dry, hard fudge. Too little beating and the fudge will be flat and dense. The right amount of beating introduces just enough air into the mixture to produce fudge with the consistency that makes it melt in your mouth.

Finally, presentation is important. A professional fudge-maker will tell you that "good fudge has no end." That means the customer wants to buy a piece from the middle of the batch. After it is molded, the ends of the batch are often cut off but are not sold, instead becoming the free samples that most stores place out for passers-by.

ATTRACTIONS

How to Use the Attraction Guide

Following is an alphabetical guide to Dells area attractions. Each listing includes the address and phone number, as well as the following information: (a) *Type of activity:* a very brief description of the type of attraction. (b) *Area:* similar to the listings for lodging, the general vicinity of the attraction. (c) *Cost:* listed is the projected "sticker" cost (before any discounts) for this coming summer. We have taken the liberty of guessing a bit, since prices from one year to another tend to vary by a small amount, if at all. Also, costs are rounded, as some Dells attractions have a knack for oddball prices, like $13.27. We rounded up odd amounts to the nearest half dollar. (d) *Author's rating:* This is the subjective rating of the author and research team. It reflects our own opinion about a particular attraction. (e) *Kid, teen, adult, and senior ratings:* These are ratings by a sampling of kids (defined as kindergarten through grade school), teens (ages 12 through 19 were sampled, but their opinions probably reflect many young adults through mid-twenties as well), adults (for our purposes, we sampled ages 25 through 55), and seniors (we sampled ages 55 and up). (f) *Rainy day activity:* If the weather is chilly and/or rainy, is this activity still possible? Rainy day activities can be a subjective matter— for instance, a ride on the ducks may be available on rainy days, but it may not be nearly as enjoyable in a downpour. In these cases, we gave the attraction a "yes," but with additional comment, such as, "more enjoyable on pleasant days." (g) *Comments:* A brief, and sometimes not so brief, comment from the author.

Following this alphabetical listing of attractions are some important cross-listings to help you find the best activities to meet your personal interests. We list attractions by category, and we give touring tips on water parks and attractions. Finally we suggest some half-day and full-day combinations that will help you to enjoy a variety of activities in a limited amount of time.

Adare Go Karts
1830 Wisconsin Dells Parkway
608-253-7170
Type of Activity: Go-kart Track
Area: Dells Parkway
Cost: $4.50/ride list price
Author's Rating: ☆☆
Kid Rating: ☆☆
Teen Rating: ☆☆
Adult Rating: ☆
Senior Rating: 1/2
Rainy Day Activity: No
Comments: Outdone by Big Chief and Crazy King Ludwig, but Adare is still an OK ride.

Adventure Zone
212 Broadway
608-254-4752
Type of Activity: Arcade/virtual reality/simulators
Area: Broadway
Cost: $5 for 20 tokens
Author's Rating: ☆☆
Kid Rating: ☆☆☆
Teen Rating: ☆☆☆
Adult Rating: ☆☆
Senior Rating: 1/2
Rainy Day Activity: Yes
Comments: Interesting and fun arcade, and a good place to try if you've never experienced virtual reality. Keep in mind that the more sophisticated VR experiences are a bit pricey.

Adventurer's Excitement Center
Broadway
Type of Activity: Motion simulator
Area: Broadway
Cost: Adults and children $5, seniors $4
Author's Rating: ☆☆
Kid Rating: ☆☆
Teen Rating: ☆☆☆
Adult Rating: ☆☆☆
Senior Rating: ☆☆

Rainy Day Activity: Yes
Comments: If you have never experienced a simulator before, it's worth a try. Like other simulators, this one uses the same technology as sophisticated flight trainers used to train pilots. Basically, simulators combine synchronized movement of your cabin and a realistic motion picture to give a very real sensation of speed and movement. Worthwhile, but a bit pricey for a ride lasting only a few minutes.

Air Boingo Bungee Jump
1450 Wisconsin Dells Parkway
608-253-5867
Type of Activity: Bungee Jump
Area: Dells Parkway
Cost: $25 first jump, $20 second jump (if you're still willing!)—also, second person from same party qualifies for $20 price
Author's Rating: ☆☆
Kid Rating: Not recommended for children
Teen Rating: ☆☆1/2
Adult Rating: ☆
Senior Rating: 1/2
Rainy Day Activity: No
Comments: A thrill for teen daredevils and (at least in the author's opinion) insane adults.

B&H Trout Farm
3640 Highway 13
608-254-7280
Type of Activity: Fishing
Area: Highway 13 North
Cost: $2 adults, $1 under 14, plus pay for fish by the inch
Author's Rating: ☆☆
Kid Rating: ☆☆
Teen Rating: 1/2
Adult Rating: ☆☆
Senior Rating: ☆☆

Rainy Day Activity: No
Comments: Good place to visit for the angler in your group. Poles and bait are furnished and no fishing license is required. Important advantage for the squeamish—B&H will also clean your catch. Open 8 A.M. to 8 P.M. in season.

Badger Helicopters
633 Wisconsin Dells Parkway North
608-254-4880
Type of Activity: Helicopter Tour
Area: Parkway at Olde Kilbourn Amusements
Cost: Varies, $15 and up.
Author's Rating: ☆☆
Kid Rating: ☆☆
Teen Rating: ☆☆1/2
Adult Rating: ☆1/2
Senior Rating: ☆
Rainy Day Activity: No
Comments: One of two helicopter tours in Dells.

Beaver Springs Fishing Park
600 Trout Road
608-254-2735

Beaver Springs Horseback Riding
600 Trout Road
608-254-2707
Type of Activity: Riding, fishing and canoe rental
Area: Trout Road south just off Highway 13
Cost: Fish priced by the inch, horseback rides about $11 and up
Author's Rating: ☆☆
Kid Rating: ☆☆
Teen Rating: ☆
Adult Rating: ☆☆
Senior Rating: ☆☆
Rainy Day Activity: No

Comments: If outdoor fun is what you're looking for, this place provides several outdoor activities for one very short car drive. Combined with the adjacent public aquarium, this complex is bliss for those interested in fishing.

Beaver Springs Public Aquarium
600 Trout Road, adjacent to fishing park and riding stable
Type of Activity: Live fish and stuffed wildlife display
Area: Trout Road south off Highway 13
Cost: $4
Author's Rating: ☆
Kid Rating: 1/2
Teen Rating: 1/2
Adult Rating: ☆
Senior Rating: ☆
Rainy Day Activity: Yes
Comments: A modest display of trout and other local fish, as well as stuffed displays of beaver and a wolf. If Upper Midwest fish and wildlife are of particular interest, it's worth the price of admission, but for the average person, not a particularly good value.

H.H. Bennett Photography Studio
215 Broadway
608-253-2261
Type of Activity: Museum of historical Dells area photography
Area: Broadway
Cost: No charge for admission
Author's Rating: ☆☆☆
Kid Rating: ☆
Teen Rating: ☆
Adult Rating: ☆☆1/2
Senior Rating: ☆☆☆
Rainy Day Activity: Yes
Comments: Adults and seniors will really appreciate this interesting, historical view of the Dells. In our opinion, this is perhaps the most overlooked but

worthwhile exhibit in the Dells area. Some good news and bad news about this attraction: the State Historical Society recently assumed ownership of the foundation and will manage the site in the future. The takeover includes substantial refurbishing of the building and museum, which will result in this attraction being closed through 1999. When it re-opens in May, 2000, this attraction should be better than ever.

Big Chief Karts & Coasters

Two Locations: (1) Highway A, just east of Dells Parkway (karts only), (2) On Dells Parkway (coasters and karts)
608-254-2490
Type of Activity: Go-karts and roller coasters
Area: Dells Parkway and just east
Cost: About $4.50 per ride
Author's Rating: ☆☆1/2
Kid Rating: ☆☆☆
Teen Rating: ☆☆☆
Adult Rating: ☆☆1/2
Senior Rating: ☆1/2
Rainy Day Activity: No
Comments: Big Chief is definitely the big chief of go-karts and coasters in the Dells with at least 14 tracks and three roller coasters. At least one of the coasters has been nationally recognized by roller coaster riding associations (yes, there is such a thing) and the cart tracks are visually impressive. The Highway A location is just a short walk off Dells Parkway.

Big Sky Twin Drive-in Theater

Highway 16 East
608-254-6598
Type of Activity:
Outdoor Movie Theater
Area: Highway 16 East

Cost: $6 adults, $2 under 12, ages 4 and under free, seniors $5.
Author's Rating: ☆
Kid Rating: ☆☆
Teen Rating: ☆☆
Adult Rating: ☆☆
Senior Rating: ☆☆
Rainy Day Activity: Possibly, but less enjoyable
Comments: It lives! Just like a monster from a B-movie, this drive-in theater has been difficult to kill off. If you want to give yourself, or the kids, a taste of nostalgia, catch a double feature at the Big Sky. But be warned—the drive-in may also bring back memories of mosquitoes, the rearview mirror blocking a part of the movie screen, trudging for (what seemed like) miles to go to the restroom, and lousy sound. What did you say was on TV in the motel room tonight?

Bill Nehring's
Haunted Dungeon of Horror

Broadway
Type of Activity: Haunted house
Area: Uptown
Cost: $4 adults
Author's Rating: ☆
Kid Rating: ☆
Teen Rating: ☆☆
Adult Rating: ☆
Senior Rating: ☆
Rainy Day Activity: Yes
Comments: A pretty good time, but out-done by other haunted house attractions.

Canyon Creek Riding Stable

Highway 12 and Hillman Road
608-253-6942
Type of Activity: Horseback Riding
Area: Just off Highway 12 in Lake Delton
Cost: Varies

Author's Rating: ☆☆
Kid Rating: ☆☆
Teen Rating: ☆☆
Adult Rating: ☆1/2
Senior Rating: ☆
Rainy Day Activity: No
Comments: Nice location and pleasant trails make this an enjoyable place to ride.

Chalet Lanes

740 Oak Street
608-254-8727
Type of Activity: Bowling
Area: Broadway
Cost: Typical bowling line rates
Author's Rating: ☆☆
Kid Rating: ☆☆
Teen Rating: ☆☆
Adult Rating: ☆
Senior Rating: ☆
Rainy Day Activity: Yes
Comments: Small bowling center with lounge and grill.

Christmas Mountain Golf Course

8944 Christmas Mountain Road
Tee times call 608-254-3971,
condo reservations call 800-289-1066
Type of Activity: Golf course
Area: Exit 87, Highway H west of I-90, catch Highway H at stoplight on Highway 13
Cost: In season, weekends $44, weekdays $40, includes cart; seniors get 10% discount
Author's Rating: ☆☆1/2
Kid Rating: NA
Teen Rating: NA
Adult Rating: ☆☆1/2 for golfers
Senior Rating: ☆☆1/2 for golfers
Rainy Day Activity: No

Comments: This course, located just west of the Dells, is unspectacular but has some appeal. If a memorable round of golf is your goal, choose Trapper's Turn; if not, Christmas Mountain offers a more economical alternative. Golf packages including a condo stay are available.

Circus World Museum

426 Water Street, Baraboo
608-356-0800
Web Page: www.cwbaraboo.org
Type of Activity: Museum and (during summer) performing circus
Area: About 15 minutes from the Dells in Baraboo area on Highway 113
Cost: $13 for adults, $7 for children 3–12, during May to early September live performance period; other times $4 for adults, $2 for children, Senior discounts.
Author's Rating: ☆☆1/2
Kid Rating: ☆☆
Teen Rating: ☆1/2
Adult Rating: ☆☆1/2
Senior Rating: ☆☆1/2
Rainy Day Activity: Yes, but not ideal in rainy weather
Comments: Operated by the State of Wisconsin, this is considered one of the premiere displays of circus memorabilia in the U.S. During peak tourist time (May through early September), Circus World brings in a variety of excellent live circus acts for two or three performances daily. Educational and fun for those with even a passing interest in the circus. Pick up a flyer at tourist information racks for a daily schedule of performances, or call recorded information line at 608-356-0800.

Henry Hamilton Bennett

A Civil War injury not only changed the life of H.H. Bennett, but may have been one of the main reasons why Wisconsin Dells became a major tourist spot. As a soldier during the Civil War, Bennett sustained a serious injury that made it impossible for him to continue his pre-war career of professional carpentry. Back from the war, he was desperate to find a way to earn a living, and turned to photography.

Mechanically gifted, Bennett built many of his own cameras. He is credited with building the first stop-action shutter camera. But he also had a gift for capturing the beauty of the Dells scenery. For over forty years, Bennett traveled throughout the Dells area and recorded the sights on film. His early efforts included many stereoscopic photos, which were a popular form of entertainment at that time. Stereoscopic photos were three-dimensional photos, like Viewmaster photos are today, and these photos were wildly popular during the 1800s and early 1900s. Bennett's Dells shots were a national sensation, and are often credited for making the Dells a popular tourist attraction. Perhaps Bennett's most famous photograph was of a man jumping over a chasm from one rock to another, a feat which today is performed only by trained dogs.

Bennett is credited for developing many advances in photography and photographic equipment. His innovations in shutters allowed him to capture action such as his famous man leaping picture. Some people credit Bennett with inventing the art of photo journalism during 1886 when he published a series of photos documenting the life of raftsmen as they took their lumber down the Wisconsin River.

Today, much of Bennett's equipment and photo work has been preserved by the H.H. Bennett Studio Foundation and is on display in a museum located on Broadway. Included in the collection are more than 5,000 glass plate negatives as well as several hand-made cameras. The museum was recently named an official site by the Wisconsin State Historical Society, and that organization will remodel the museum and manage it after it re-opens. Because of the remodeling, the museum is expected to be closed during most of 1999, to re-open in May, 2000.

Coldwater Canyon Golf Course

4065 River Road
Tee times call 608-254-8489
Type of Activity: Golf course (9 holes)
Area: River Road two miles north of
Wisconsin Dells, near Chula Vista
Cost: In season, approximately $18
Author's Rating: ☆☆
Kid Rating: NA
Teen Rating: NA
Adult Rating: ☆☆for golfers
Senior Rating: ☆☆for golfers
Rainy Day Activity: No
Comments: This course, which was orig-
inally built in the 1920s, plays nicely. If
a memorable round of golf is your goal,
choose Trapper's Turn, but if you want
to catch a pleasant nine holes, Coldwater
Canyon offers a more economical alter-
native.

Corny Maze/Go-karts/ Basketball "Golf"

564 Wisconsin Dells Parkway South
608-253-7332
Type of Activity: go-kart track, maze
and basketball shooting game
Area: Highway 12
Cost: About $4 per activity
Author's Rating: ☆
Kid Rating: ☆1/2
Teen Rating: ☆1/2
Adult Rating: ☆
Senior Rating: ☆
Rainy Day Activity: No
Comments: A little outclassed by other
area attractions, this small entertainment
complex has a so-so go-kart track,
human maze, and a basketball shooting
game. An OK place to visit if it's con-
venient and time permits, but not worth
a special trip.

Country Legends Music Theater

Type of Activity: Music theater
Phone: 608-253-5357
Area: the Parkway
Author's Rating: ☆
Kid Rating: ☆
Teen Rating: ☆
Adult Rating: ☆☆
Senior Rating: ☆☆
Rainy Day Activity: Yes
Comments: Shows at 3 P.M. and 8 P.M.
feature a country music review. Call for
prices.

Crystal Grand Music Theater

430 Munroe Street
254-4545/800-696-7999
Type of Activity: Music Theater
Area: Munroe Street
Cost: depends on performer
Author's Rating: ☆☆
Kid Rating: ☆
Teen Rating: ☆
Adult Rating: ☆☆
Senior Rating: ☆☆
Rainy Day Activity: Yes
Comments: This theater brings in well-
known performers and music acts,
leaning toward country, old time rock
and roll, and standards. Recent acts have
included Roger Whittaker, Frankie Valli
and the Four Seasons, Willie Nelson, and
George Carlin. Call for performance
schedule.

CyberMind Virtual Reality Center

Broadway
Type of Activity:
Virtual reality/simulator
Area: Broadway
Cost: Approximately $5 per activity
Author's Rating: ☆☆

Kid Rating: ☆☆1/2
Teen Rating: ☆☆1/2
Adult Rating: ☆1/2
Senior Rating: ☆1/2
Rainy Day Activity: Yes
Comments: A good place to try if you've never experienced virtual reality. Be warned that the more sophisticated VR attractions and simulators tend to be a bit pricey, about $5 per person for a ride lasting two or three minutes.

Dells Arcade

119 Broadway
608-254-8568
Type of Activity: Arcade
Area: Uptown Dells
Cost: $1 for 4 tokens
Author's Rating: ☆☆
Kid Rating: ☆☆☆
Teen Rating: ☆☆☆
Adult Rating: ☆☆
Senior Rating: ☆
Rainy Day Activity: Yes
Comments: One of a number of arcades and similar attractions in uptown Dells.

Dells Auto Museum

591 Wisconsin Dells Parkway
608-254-2008
Type of Activity: Museum
Area: The Parkway
Cost: $4, seniors $3
Author's Rating: ☆☆
Kid Rating: ☆
Teen Rating: ☆1/2
Adult Rating: ☆☆
Senior Rating: ☆☆
Rainy Day Activity: Yes
Comments: Some interesting autos displayed. This should be high on the list for auto buffs.

Dells Boat Tours

11 Broadway
608-254-8555
Web: www.dells.com/boattour.html
Type of Activity: Boat tour
Area: Uptown
Cost: Approximately $10 to $16 for adults, $6 to $9 children, 5 and under free (see comments)
Author's Rating: ☆☆☆
Kid Rating: ☆☆
Teen Rating: ☆☆
Adult Rating: ☆☆☆
Senior Rating: ☆☆☆
Rainy Day Activity: Yes, but somewhat less pleasant in inclement weather
Comments: A Dells Boat Tour is one of the classic Dells attractions that every visitor should experience at least once. In our opinion, the front of the Upper Dells dock building on Broadway is one of the grandest looking buildings in the Dells area. Two tours are offered: the Lower Dells tour is shorter, about an hour, while the Upper Dells tour makes two shore landings, allowing passengers to take brief walking tours, and takes about two hours. The Lower Dells tour is the least costly ticket, about $9 for adults and $6 for children. Upper Dells tickets are about $13 and $7. Combined tickets, at about $16 for adults and $9 for kids, are a good deal if you're up for two boat rides (which leave from different docks, requiring you to either drive, take a free shuttle, or hike a fair distance to the other dock). If your schedule permits only one ride, the Upper Dells is our recommendation.

Dells Ducks
(a.k.a. "Original WWII Ducks")

Wisconsin Dells Parkway, tickets available on Highway 12 and uptown (look for the Red, White and Blue Duck)
Type of Activity: Land and water tour riding on Red, White and Blue ducks
Area: Dock located on Dells Parkway
Cost: Approximately $11 adults, $8 children
Author's Rating: ☆☆☆
Kid Rating: ☆☆1/2
Teen Rating: ☆☆
Adult Rating: ☆☆
Senior Rating: ☆☆1/2
Rainy Day Activity: Yes, but less pleasant in inclement weather
Comments: With two duck companies operating in the Dells, you have to be on your toes to realize that "Original WWII Ducks" and "Original Ducks" are not operated by the same firm. A better way to keep them straight is that these ducks are the red, white and blue ducks, not the green and white ducks. If you buy your tickets at a place other than the duck dock, save yourself time and embarrassment by knowing from which company you bought tickets, so you don't "quack everybody up" when you try to board the wrong duck. By the way, a "duck" is a World War II amphibious vehicle, modified to carry about 20 tourists on land and water around the Dells on a one hour-plus tour. Ducks are perfect vehicles for Dells touring, and kids get a kick out of the duck entering the water with an impressive splash. Which color duck is better? It's a close call—our research team gives the edge to the green and whites, but only by a nose (or in this case, a bill). Another question: is a duck ride a substitute for a boat tour? Doing both is a little repetitive, but ducks and

boats do view somewhat different sights and provide different experiences. If you have time, we suggest at least one boat tour and a duck tour. If pressed for time, and you have grade-school children in your group, the ducks offer a water-land change of pace that seems to keep that age group more interested. If you don't have kids in your group, flip a coin to choose a boat or duck tour, and save the other for next time.

Dells Mining Company

Wisconsin Dells Parkway
608-253-7002
Type of Activity: Find your own treasure
Area: Dells Parkway
Cost: $9 plus extras
Author's Rating: ☆1/2
Kid Rating: ☆1/2
Teen Rating: ☆1/2
Adult Rating: ☆/2
Senior Rating: ☆1/2
Rainy Day Activity: Yes
Comments: Yes, you do pay to trawl for treasure. Then, if you want your treasure mounted you pay even more. $9 allows you to dig for treasure—you get to keep whatever you find—usually these are inexpensive stones, but there is a small chance of finding a more valuable stone.

Devil's Lake State Park

About 2 miles south of Baraboo, follow Highway 12 to Hwy 159 East
608-356-8301
The most popular of three state parks in the area, Devil's Lake offers many campsites, a nice beach, biking, and hiking, including a neat trail winding up the side of a cliff. One of the most popular parks in Wisconsin in terms of attendance. Phone reservations for one of the park's 400+ campsites may be made between June 1 and August 31.

Splash into fun and adventure on an original Wisconsin Duck. A 7½ mile tour on land and water gives visitors a unique view of Wisconsin Dells. Breathtaking scenery and thrilling water entrances highlight this enjoyable ride. The Wisconsin Ducks are open mid-May through mid-October.

Elusive Dream Balloons

(608) 586-5737
Cost: $175 per person
Call for more information
and appointment.

Extreme World

Wisconsin Dells Parkway
Type of Activity: Cluster of hair-
raising, action-oriented activities
Area: Dells Parkway
Cost: Depends on activity
Author's Rating: ☆☆
Kid Rating: ☆☆
Teen Rating: ☆☆☆
Adult Rating: ☆☆
Senior Rating: ☆
Rainy Day Activity: No
Comments: Activities include bungee
jump, skycoaster (a two-seat bungee
contraption), karts, "Alligator Alley,"
"Haunted Safari," and paintball.

Family Land

Wisconsin Dells Parkway
608-254-7766
Type of Activity: Water Park
Area: Dells Parkway
Cost: $18 for all inclusive pass, $8 for
second day, but coupons are abundant,
and entry after 5:00 P.M. may be half-
price.
Author's Rating: ☆☆1/2
Kid Rating: ☆☆☆
Teen Rating: ☆☆1/2
Adult Rating: ☆☆1/2
Senior Rating: ☆1/2
Rainy Day Activity: No
Comments: Although it has been
dwarfed by Noah's Ark, Family Land
remains a nice Dells attraction, combining about ten waterslide attractions and
a wave pool with some fun out-of-water
attractions that are especially appealing
to kids. It's a more economical choice

than Noah's Ark, but with far fewer
slides. See touring tips section for touring suggestions regarding all the water
parks.

Fast Track Go-karts

Highway 16
608-253-6090
Type of Activity: Go-kart track
Area: out of town, Highway 16
Cost: $5, coupons available for $1 off
Author's Rating: ☆☆
Kid Rating: ☆☆
Teen Rating: ☆☆
Adult Rating: ☆☆
Senior Rating: ☆
Rainy Day Activity: No
Comments: One of several choices for
go-kart driving in the Dells area, this
choice is on Highway 16. Unless
this happens to be a convenient location
for you, there is no compelling reason to
travel outside of town with many closer
go-kart choices available.

Game Zone

1000 Stand Rock Road
608-254-8386
Type of Activity: Arcade
Area: Stand Rock Road is on the hill
just north of Highway 13 west of
the river
Cost: $1 for 4 tokens
Author's Rating: ☆☆
Kid Rating: ☆☆1/2
Teen Rating: ☆☆1/2
Adult Rating: ☆☆
Senior Rating: ☆
Rainy Day Activity: Yes
Comments: This arcade is convenient to
the Timber Falls complex and a number
of restaurants, so it's a perfect place to
part with any leftover lunch or dinner
money, or to unwind after a stressful
round of mini-golf.

Haunted Mansion of Baldazar
112 Broadway
608-254-7513
Type of Activity: Haunted House
Area: Uptown
Cost: $5, 12 and under $4
Author's Rating: ☆1/2
Kid Rating: ☆☆
Teen Rating: ☆☆
Adult Rating: ☆1/2
Senior Rating: ☆
Rainy Day Activity: Yes
Comments: A pretty well-done haunted house, with several chambers that scare and surprise. May be somewhat intense for the little ones; a good test is the entrance area, which can be viewed without admission. If the sights there intimidate a child, take a pass on this attraction.

Ho-Chunk Casino & Bingo
Highway 12, West of Lake Delton
608-356-6210
Bingo Information Line
800-362-8404
Type of Activity: Gambling casino and live entertainment
Area: Just off Highway 12 between Lake Delton and Baraboo
Cost: Who knows, you may end up winning!
Author's Rating: ☆☆1/2
Kid Rating: NA
Teen Rating: NA
Adult Rating: ☆☆
Senior Rating: ☆☆☆
Rainy Day Activity: Yes
Comments: A nice gambling casino and bingo parlor. The attached restaurant serves lackluster food, even by Dells standards, and the casino has occasional live entertainment. You must be 18 or older to enter, and ID's are checked regularly. The primary gambling is blackjack and slot machines.

Holiday Shores Marina and Boat Rental
3900 River Road
608-254-2878
Call for rates on boat rentals

International Crane Foundation
E11376 Shady Lane Road, Baraboo
608-356-9462
Type of Activity: Live display of cranes and tour
Area: Just off Highway 12 between Lake Delton and Baraboo
Cost: $7 adults, $6 seniors, $3 for ages 11 and under
Author's Rating: ☆☆☆
Kid Rating: ☆☆
Teen Rating: ☆
Adult Rating: ☆☆1/2
Senior Rating: ☆☆1/2
Rainy Day Activity: No
Comments: Operated by the International Crane Foundation, this attraction shows these beautiful birds in their natural habitat, as well as informing visitors about cranes. The ICF has done a magnificent job of helping to restore the crane population, and has done an equally commendable job in making this an interesting and worthwhile attraction. Guided tours are at 10 A.M., 1 P.M. and 3 P.M. but you can tour on your own if those times aren't convenient. A picnic area is available, and the setting is very pleasant.

J.B. Helicopters
Highway 12 & 13 at Pirate's Cove
608-254-6381
Type of Activity: Helicopter tour
Area: Stand Rock Road is on the hill just north of Highway 13 west of the river
Cost: Varies, allow minimum of $15
Author's Rating: ☆☆
Kid Rating: ☆☆

Teen Rating: ☆☆
Adult Rating: ☆☆
Senior Rating: ☆☆
Rainy Day Activity: No
Comments: This helicopter ride departs from the hilltop near Pirate's Cove mini-golf, and provides a unique way to see the sights.

King Ludwig's Adventure Park
1851 Wisconsin Dells Parkway
608-254-5464
Type of Activity: Go-kart Track, Batting Cage, Boat Tag, Arcade
Area: The Parkway
Cost: $4.50 a ride for go-karts and boat tag, $1 for 13 balls in batting cage, $20 per person for Skyscraper ride, day passes available.
Author's Rating: ☆☆1/2
Kid Rating: ☆☆☆
Teen Rating: ☆☆☆
Adult Rating: ☆☆
Senior Rating: ☆
Rainy Day Activity: Indoor arcade only
Comments: A major attraction for older kids and teens, one of the most happening places on the Parkway. New in 1998, Skyscraper soars to 185 feet with two-person open-air seats at each end of a rotating arm.

Lake Delton Water Sports
Location 1. Highway 12
Location 2. Hiawatha Drive
608-254-8702
Call for rates on rentals of boats and jet skis.

Laser Storm
501 Broadway
608-254-4855
Type of Activity: Laser tag game
Area: Broadway
Cost: $5.50, discounts for multiple games played
Author's Rating: ☆☆
Kid Rating: ☆☆
Teen Rating: ☆☆☆
Adult Rating: ☆
Senior Rating: 1/2
Rainy Day Activity: Yes
Comments: Laser tag is a simulated battle in which participants of one team trying to gain strategic position to blast members from other teams with lasers. Participants wear special vests which record hits, and scores are kept electronically. Our feeling is that this is a little too wild for older adults and seniors, but a good attraction for pre-teens and teens. Since competition is intense, younger children may feel overwhelmed if they are matched against older kids.

Lost Canyon Tours
720 Canyon Road
608-254-8757
Type of Activity: Wagon ride
Area: Canyon Road, just off Adams, which is off of Highway 12
Cost: $5.50 for adults, $3 for under age 12, ages 3 and under free
Author's Rating: ☆☆1/2
Kid Rating: ☆☆1/2
Teen Rating: ☆1/2
Adult Rating: ☆☆1/2
Senior Rating: ☆☆
Rainy Day Activity: No
Comments: A half-hour tour on a horse-pulled wagon through very scenic rock formations. A one-of-a-kind Dells attraction that's interesting and fun. Tours leave about four times each hour until 7:30 p.m. A picnic area with grills, beach, and snack shop is available.

Mark Twain Yacht Tour

Wisconsin Dells Parkway
608-254-6080
Type of Activity: Boat excursion
Area: Buy tickets and shuttle from
WWII (red, white and blue) Duck
dock, shuttle to dock
Cost: Approximately $10 adults
Author's Rating: ☆☆
Kid Rating: ☆☆
Teen Rating: ☆
Adult Rating: ☆☆
Senior Rating: ☆☆1/2
Rainy Day Activity: Yes
Comments: This one-hour boat tour of
the Upper Dells does not include land-
ings, but does allow you to view many
beautiful formations from the yacht.
Tours depart at 10 A.M., noon, 2 P.M. and
4 p.m. It is important to buy your ticket
and be ready to board the shuttle one-
half hour before the scheduled departure
times.

Mass Panic

Wisconsin Dells Parkway &
County Highway A
Type of Activity: "Fun" House
Area: The Parkway
Cost: Approximately $6 adults and teens
Author's Rating: ☆☆
Kid Rating: ☆☆1/2
Teen Rating: ☆☆1/2
Adult Rating: ☆
Senior Rating: 1/2
Rainy Day Activity: Yes
Comments: This unusual attraction is the
latest entry in the race to frighten your
children to the max.

Mid-Continent Railway

Walnut Street, North Freedom
608-522-4261
Web: www.mcrwy.com
Type of Activity: Train museum and ride
Area: North Freedom, Wisconsin

Cost: Adults $9, under 12 $5.50,
seniors $8, family $25 maximum
Author's Rating: ☆☆
Kid Rating: ☆☆
Teen Rating: ☆
Adult Rating: ☆☆
Senior Rating: ☆☆1/2
Rainy Day Activity: Yes
Comments: Four trips daily in-season.
Picnic area available. Mid-Continent
also offers rail tours to view Autumn
colors, usually during the first week in
October, as well as winter and Holiday
trains. Call or visit web site for more
information.

Nature Safaris

(see Time Travel Geologic Tours)

Mirror Lake State Park

E10320 Fern Dell Road
608-254-2333
One of three state parks in the Dells area.
Over 2,000 acres and 147 campsites.
Located roughly between Baraboo and
Lake Delton. Fairly convenient to Lake
Delton (exit 92) area.

Noah's Ark

1410 Wisconsin Dells Parkway
608-254-6351
Type of Activity: Water park
Area: Dells Parkway
Cost: Approximately $23 for
unlimited pass, $19 for seniors,
coupons and discounts pretty easy
to find
Author's Rating: ☆☆☆
Kid Rating: ☆☆☆
Teen Rating: ☆☆☆
Adult Rating: ☆☆☆
Senior Rating: ☆☆1/2
Rainy Day Activity: No

Catch a wave this summer at one of Wisconsin Dells' three world-class waterparks, featuring speed slides, water flumes, lazy river rides and kiddie activity pools.

Comments: In the past dozen years, Noah's Ark has grown from a small water park, competing on more or less equal footing with Family Land and Waterworld, to THE premiere attraction in the Dells. A spectacular new slide is added just about every year, and Noah's Ark continues to grow and improve each summer. Kids love it, teens flock to it, and it even has ardent fans among adults and seniors. We know one otherwise normal adult who travels over 100 miles to visit Noah's Ark—not just once or twice, but more than a dozen times each summer! Water parks can be physically demanding; and there is *a lot* of walking and climbing stairs as well as swimming. If you are up to the task physically and aren't adverse to the water, Noah's Ark is a place you should not miss.

No Fly Zone
505 W. Broadway
608-742-5537
Type of Activity: Arcade, virtual reality, and simulators
Area: Uptown
Cost: Call for rates
Author's Rating: ☆☆
Kid Rating: ☆☆
Teen Rating: ☆☆☆
Adult Rating: ☆☆
Senior Rating: ☆
Rainy Day Activity: Yes
Comments: Virtual reality as a technology is still in its infancy, and national market research shows that many adults are disappointed, and even become a little nauseous, with the experience. However, virtual reality centers thrive in tourist areas, and you may want to decide for yourself if virtual is as good as the real thing. The experience can be a little hard on your wallet, at about $5 per person for a two- or three-minute VR experience. If you're really up to it, try the looping roller coaster simulator—but heed the attendants warning to empty your pockets before you ride!

OK Corral Riding Stable
Highway 16
800-254-2811

Olde Kilbourn Amusements
633 Wisconsin Dells Parkway
608-254-2127
Type of Activity: Go-karts, mini-golf, and bumper boats
Area: The Parkway
Cost: $4 per ride
Author's Rating: ☆1/2
Kid Rating: ☆☆
Teen Rating: ☆1/2
Adult Rating: ☆☆
Senior Rating: ☆
Rainy Day Activity: No
Comments: Among go-kart tracks and mini-golf on the strip, this is the budget choice. Not bad for kids who are just getting started in their go-kart driving or mini-golf careers, but compared to Big Chief, Crazy King Ludwig's, and the rest, Olde Kilbourn is—well—*old*.

Old River Mini-Golf
Eddy Street
608-254-8336
Type of Activity: Mini-golf
Area: Just off Broadway uptown, across the street from the Upper Dells Boat Docks
Cost: $5, second round one-half price
Author's Rating: ☆☆
Kid Rating: ☆☆
Teen Rating: ☆☆
Adult Rating: ☆☆
Senior Rating: ☆☆1/2
Rainy Day Activity: No
Comments: Although not nearly as spectacular as some of the other mini-golf

places, Old River has a sort of charm to it. Seniors may appreciate the flat terrain as compared to the larger mini-golf complexes, which are built on steep hills. Here's a great way to spend three to five hours in the uptown area: Park on Eddy Street (just off Broadway), take the Upper Dells boat tour, walk around uptown for a bit (maybe catch lunch and take in Ripley's Believe It Or Not or the Haunted Mansion), try a simulated ride at Adventurer Excitement Center or No-Fly Zone, and then hit Old River for a round of mini-golf.

Original Wisconsin Ducks
Wisconsin Dells Parkway
608-254-8751
Type of Activity: Land and water tour in Green and White ducks
Area: Dells Parkway
Cost: $14 for adults, $9 for under age 12, free for age 5 and under, $11 for seniors
Author's Rating: ☆☆☆
Kid Rating: ☆☆1/2
Teen Rating: ☆☆
Adult Rating: ☆☆1/2
Senior Rating: ☆☆
Rainy Day Activity: Yes, but more enjoyable in good weather
Comments: A duck ride is traditionally a "must" Dells experience. For more general information on duck rides, see the Dells Ducks entry (page 66).

Pirate's Cove Mini-Golf
Highways 12-13-16-23 Intersection
608-254-8336
Type of Activity: Mini-golf
Area: Highway 13 at north end of the Parkway
Cost: $6, second round one-half price
Author's Rating: ☆☆1/2
Kid Rating: ☆☆1/2

Teen Rating: ☆☆1/2
Adult Rating: ☆☆1/2
Senior Rating: ☆☆1/2
Rainy Day Activity: No
Comments: Ahoy, mates! If mini-golf is your game, here are not just18 holes, but *five* different 18-hole mini-golf courses, winding among countless waterfalls on an attractive hillside landscape. A couple of years back, Pirate's Cove added a "family fun area" that includes a nice little playground and picnic area. Use of this area is free to families who play a round of golf.

Point Bluff Canoe Rental
3199 County Road Z
608-253-6181

Ranch Riding Stable
S944 Christmas Mountain Road/ Highway H
608-254-3935
Type of Activity: Horseback riding, wagon rides and petting zoo
Area: near Christmas Mountain resort
Cost: $7 adults, $4.50 for 12 and under, free for 5 and under
Author's Rating: ☆
Kid Rating: ☆☆
Teen Rating: ☆
Adult Rating: ☆☆
Senior Rating: ☆
Rainy Day Activity: No
Comments: A little out of the way for most Dells visitors, but has nice trails through wooded and meadow areas.

Ripley's Believe It Or Not
115 Broadway
608-253-7556
Type of Activity: Museum
Area: Broadway, uptown Dells
Cost: $7 adults, $4.50 for 12 and under, free for 5 and under

Author's Rating: ☆☆/2
Kid Rating: ☆☆
Teen Rating: ☆☆1/2
Adult Rating: ☆☆1/2
Senior Rating: ☆☆
Rainy Day Activity: Yes
Comments: The Dells version of Ripley's includes some wonderfully bizarre exhibits. If you've visited Ripley's in Orlando or elsewhere, you'll probably find this one to be a bit of a letdown, but it's still great fun and a good way to burn about an hour, especially on a rainy day.

Riverside & Great Northern Railway Preservation Society

N115 County Road N
(Follow Stand Rock Road north about one mile from Dells)
608-254-6367
Type of Activity: Train ride
Area: North of town
Cost: $5 adults, $4 seniors,
$3 for ages 5-14, free for 5 and under
Author's Rating: ☆☆1/2
Kid Rating: ☆☆
Teen Rating: ☆1/2
Adult Rating: ☆☆1/2
Senior Rating: ☆☆1/2
Rainy Day Activity: Yes, but rain diminishes the fun
Comments: A 30-minute train ride on a 15-inch (narrower than standard track) railroad.

Riverview Park and Waterworld

Wisconsin Dells Parkway
608-254-2608
Type of Activity: Water park and amusement rides
Area: Dells Parkway
Cost: $15 all-activity pass, 5 and under $9, water-only pass is less, twilight all-activity pass is $9, coupons are available, free

observation. Under age 3 free for water-only attractions.
Author's Rating: ☆☆
Kid Rating: ☆☆1/2
Teen Rating: ☆☆1/2
Adult Rating: ☆☆
Senior Rating: ☆☆
Rainy Day Activity: No
Comments: To stand out from Noah's Ark, Riverview Park & Waterworld features carnival-type rides and roller coaster as well as some water attractions, with special attention paid to small kiddies. A fun house, carousel, and other attractions are geared toward little ones, and there are some teen-oriented rides as well. If your main interest is a water park, Noah's Ark is a better choice, but if you are seeking a little water as well as carnival rides and activities, consider Riverview Park & Waterworld.

Rocky Arbor State Park

Highways 12-16 North
608-254-8001
The smallest (only 225 acres) of three state parks in the area. With 89 campsites and the most convenient location to Dells attractions, this is a park campers may want to consider.

Serpent Safari

1425 Wisconsin Dells Parkway
608-253-3200
Type of Activity: Reptile zoo and exhibits
Area: Dells Parkway, in strip mall at entrance to the Raintree Resort
Cost: $6 for adults, $5 for seniors, $4 for ages 12 and under
Author's Rating: ☆☆1/2
Kid Rating: ☆☆1/2
Teen Rating: ☆☆1/2
Adult Rating: ☆☆1/2
Senior Rating: ☆☆1/2
Rainy Day Activity: Yes

Comments: What did Indiana Jones say? "Snakes . . . why do there always have to be snakes!" The Dells has snakes, and some other reptiles too, at Serpent Safari. Unique, fun, educational, and a good way to spend an hour or so.

Shipwreck Lagoon Adventure Golf

213 Windy Hill Road
608-253-7772
Type of Activity: Mini-golf, batting cage, flight simulator
Area: Dells Parkway
Cost: $6 for golf, second round one-half price; $4 (children $3) for flight simulator
Author's Rating: ☆☆
Kid Rating: ☆☆
Teen Rating: ☆☆1/2
Adult Rating: ☆☆1/2
Senior Rating: ☆☆
Rainy Day Activity: No
Comments: Mini-golf combines with batting cages and a flight simulator ride.

Splatter Zone Paintball Shooting Range

Broadway
Type of Activity: Shooting arcade
Area: Broadway
Cost: Approximately $3 for a decent number of shots
Author's Rating: ☆☆
Kid Rating: ☆☆
Teen Rating: ☆☆
Adult Rating: ☆☆
Senior Rating: ☆
Rainy Day Activity: Yes
Comments: If you're strolling down Broadway and get the sudden urge to shoot paintballs at targets, stop here.

Stand Rock Indian Ceremonial

608-253-9505
Type of Activity: Traditional Native American Ceremonial
Area: Four miles north of Wisconsin Dells, north on Stand Rock Road off Highway 16
Cost: Reserved seating $15, general admission $13, age 6 and under free
Author's Rating: ☆☆
Kid Rating: ☆☆
Teen Rating: ☆☆
Adult Rating: ☆☆
Senior Rating: ☆☆
Rainy Day Activity: No
Comments: The show is held daily from mid-June to Labor Day starting at 8:45 p.m. Part of the allure of this show is the setting: It's held in a natural stone amphitheater near the west bank of the Wisconsin River. Attire and dances are authentic, and not only is the local Ho-Chunk tribe represented, but guest performers present culture from their tribes. This is a long running Dells favorite and an entertaining way to learn about Indian culture.

Storybook Gardens

1500 Wisconsin Dells Parkway
608-253-2391
Type of Activity: Kid's fairy tales come to life
Area: Dells Parkway
Cost: $7 for adults, $6 for children, free for age one and under
Author's Rating: ☆☆
Kid Rating: ☆☆☆
Teen Rating: 1/2
Adult Rating: ☆☆
Senior Rating: ☆☆
Rainy Day Activity: No

Traditional dancers perform nightly during the season at the Stand Rock Indian Ceremonial.

Comments: Animated displays, live performances and kiddie rides make this a favorite of the younger set. If you visit with children in the age group that appreciates fairy tales, Storybook Gardens is an absolute must.

Timber Falls
Broadway and Stand Rock Road
608-254-4859
Type of Activity: Mini-golf
and log flume ride
Area: Just off north end of the Parkway near Kilbourn Bridge west of river
Cost: Golf $6, second round one-half price, flume ride $4, all day pass for golf and ride $15, coupons for $2 off all day pass or $1 off golf are available
Author's Rating: ☆☆1/2
Kid Rating: ☆☆1/2
Teen Rating: ☆☆☆
Adult Rating: ☆☆1/2
Senior Rating: ☆
Rainy Day Activity: No
Comments: With five different 18-hole mini-golf courses *and* a log waterslide ride, this is an entertaining place to spend a couple of hours. There's a nearby gift shop and places to eat, which is convenient. Seniors should be aware that some of the golf courses are rather hilly, with plenty of stairs to climb. Be aware that you can become at least a little wet on the log waterslide ride.

Time Travel Geologic Tours and Nature Safaris
Tours depart from Three Little Devils Scuba Shop in Devil's Lake State park
Phone 800-328-0995
Web: www.midplains.net/~peherr

Type of Activity: Guided tours of sights of geologic or natural interest in the Dells and Baraboo areas
Cost: Varies by type and length of tour, approximately $23 (adult) for a 2-1/2 hour tour
Author's Rating: ☆☆☆
Kid Rating: ☆☆
Teen Rating: ☆☆
Adult Rating: ☆☆1/2
Senior Rating: ☆☆
Rainy Day Activity: No
Comments: These unique and worthwhile guided tours include destinations of Parfrey's Glen, Devil's Lake State Park, and the Dells area. Emphasis is on natural history – including geologic formations, Indian burial mounds, old mines, and native plants. Some light hiking is involved, so wear appropriate footwear. Tours are 90 minutes and longer, and schedules and reservations can be obtained by calling the toll-free number listed above. Tours depart from Three Little Devils Scuba Shop in Devils Lake Park. Educational and entertaining.

Tommy Bartlett's Robot World & Exploratory
560 Wisconsin Dells Parkway
608-254-2525
Web: www.tommybartlett.com/
Type of Activity: Futuristic museum and interactive science playground
Area: Dells Parkway
Cost: Approximately $9 for adults, $7 for seniors, free for age 5 and under
Author's Rating: ☆☆1/2
Kid Rating: ☆☆1/2
Teen Rating: ☆☆1/2
Adult Rating: ☆☆1/2
Senior Rating: ☆☆1/2
Rainy Day Activity: Yes

Experience the feeling of astronaut weightlessness aboard the Gyrotron, one of 90 "hands-on" exhibits and displays featured at the Tommy Bartlett Robot World and Exploratory, where imagination becomes reality.

Comments: This exhibit has been updated, and in recent years has included a replica of the MIR space station (However, unlike the real one in space, the MIR in the Dells doesn't break down constantly.). Also of interest is a huge room of interactive science demonstrations, which kids who are old enough to appreciate really get a kick out of. Actually, younger kids get a kick out of them too, even though they might not care about the scientific principles involved. A wonderful place to visit on a rainy day. Visit early in the day (doors usually open at 8 A.M.) to give the kids free run of the exploratory area without having to compete with lots of other kids to get their hands on the exhibits.

Tommy Bartlett's Thrill Show
560 Wisconsin Dells Parkway
608-254-2525
Web: www.tommybartlett.com/
Type of Activity: Water ski and variety show
Area: Dells Parkway
Cost: Reserved seats about $16, first tier general admission $13, second tier general admission $10
Author's Rating: ☆☆1/2
Kid Rating: ☆☆
Teen Rating: ☆
Adult Rating: ☆☆
Senior Rating: ☆☆1/2
Rainy Day Activity: Yes, covered seating available

Comments: One of the enduring classics of the Dells is the Tommy Bartlett Thrill Show, held at 1 P.M., 4:30 P.M. and 8:30 P.M. Box office opens at 10 A.M. The show includes water and boat stunts as well as acrobats, jugglers, and other performers. Everything is done well. It's a little dated and very corny (one teen we talked to used the term "lame-ola" to describe it), but we think it's not the worst way to spend a couple of hours.

Tommy Town
1470 Wisconsin Dells Parkway
608-254-6036
Type of Activity: Fast-food eatery combined with arcade and elaborate play area
Area: Dells Parkway
Cost: Food cost plus $6 admission per child to play area; accompanying adults are free
Author's Rating: ☆☆
Kid Rating: ☆☆☆
Teen Rating: ☆☆ (arcade)
Adult Rating: NA
Senior Rating: NA
Rainy Day Activity: Yes
Comments: Combining a restaurant, arcade, and gigantic version of a fast-food restaurant playland, Tommy Town is a good time for the pre-teen crowd. Given the relative scarcity of fast food on the Parkway, Tommy Town is welcome, and although the play area is a bit pricey for what it is, it's not a bad way to spend an hour or so, especially on a rainy day.

Trapper's Turn Golf Course
652 Trapper's Turn Drive
608-253-7000
Type of Activity: Golf Course
Area: Exit 87

Cost: Peak season about $60 (includes cart) Friday-Sunday, about $54 Monday-Thursday
Author's Rating: ☆☆☆ for golfers
Kid Rating: NA
Teen Rating: NA
Adult Rating: ☆☆☆ for golfers
Senior Rating: ☆☆☆ for golfers
Rainy Day Activity: No
Comments: The premiere golf course in the Dells area, this course was designed by two-time U.S. Open champion and ESPN golf announcer Andy North. If a memorable round of golf is your goal, choose Trapper's Turn. If you're just looking to get in nine or 18 holes, try Wilderness Lodge's course, Christmas Mountain, Coldwater Canyon, or the other courses listed under "Golf" at the end of this section.

Uncle Gene's Moped Rental
1021 Stand Rock Road
608-254-6569

Wax World of the Stars
105 Broadway
608-254-2184
Type of Activity: Wax museum
Area: Broadway
Cost: $7 for adults, $4 for ages 6-12, free for ages 5 and under
Author's Rating: ☆☆
Kid Rating: ☆☆
Teen Rating: ☆☆
Adult Rating: ☆☆
Senior Rating: ☆☆
Rainy Day Activity: Yes
Comments: Visit any tourist area and you're sure to find a wax museum. The Dells version holds up pretty well compared to many other wax museums, and is pretty good fun.

Western Village

400 Broadway
Type of Activity: Entertainment
and shopping complex, includes
Chalet Cinema movie theater
Area: Broadway
Cost: $4 for mini-golf,
other activities vary
Author's Rating: ☆☆
Kid Rating: ☆☆
Teen Rating: ☆☆1/2
Adult Rating: ☆☆1/2
Senior Rating: ☆☆
Rainy Day Activity: Yes, some areas
Comments: This complex encompasses
a one-screen movie theater showing
first-run films, a modest mini-golf
course, small arcade, and numerous
shops including a tattoo parlor, psychic,
cigar shop, and eateries.

Wilderness Golf Course
(formerly Dell View)

511 E. Adams Street
608-253-4653
Type of Activity: Golf course
Area: Exit 92, Highway 12,
behind Wilderness Resort
Cost: $30 for 18 holes plus
$15 per person for cart
Author's Rating: ☆☆ for golfers
Kid Rating: NA
Teen Rating: NA
Adult Rating: ☆☆ for golfers
Senior Rating: ☆☆ for golfers
Rainy Day Activity: No
Comments: This course is not up to
Trapper's Turn in design or quality of
play, but offers a convenient and less
costly alternative. It is a relatively short
course with few memorable holes. Fair-
ways are close together, tees are a little
too close to greens, and the racket from
the Wilderness Lodge outdoor water
area detracts from the enjoyment of two
or three holes. Since the course is not too
long and fairly flat, a cart isn't a necessity, unless you feel you've already
walked enough miles in the Dells. The
course was renovated in 1998.

Wisconsin Deer Park

583 Wisconsin Dells Parkway
608-253-2041
Type of Activity: Wildlife zoo
and petting zoo
Area: Dells Parkway
Cost: $5.50 adults, $3 for ages 4-12,
free for ages 3 and under
Author's Rating: ☆☆
Kid Rating: ☆☆1/2
Teen Rating: ☆
Adult Rating: ☆☆
Senior Rating: ☆☆
Rainy Day Activity: No
Comments: Tame deer that you can pet
and feed are the attraction here, as well
as a few other animals. Kids really enjoy
getting up close and personal with
wildlife, and the experience can be
somewhat mind-blowing for pre-school
and grade school children who are from
(as we say in Wisconsin) the "Big City."

Wisconsin Dells Trout Farm
Wisconsin Dells Canoe Trips

Highway 13 and Highway K, Oxford
608-589-5353

Wisconsin Opry

E10964 Moon Road, Baraboo
608-254-7951
Type of Activity: Country
entertainment show and flea market
Area: Exit 92, Highway 12,
1/4 mile off I-90, toward Baraboo
Cost: $12 for adults, $6 for ages 6-12,
free for ages 5 and under
Author's Rating: ☆☆
Kid Rating: ☆

Teen Rating: ☆
Adult Rating: ☆☆
Senior Rating: ☆☆
Rainy Day Activity: No
Comments: Yeeeee-hah! Each night (except Sunday) at 8 o'clock. the Wisconsin Opry puts on a country music and entertainment show in the tradition of its big country cousin in Nashville. If you want to get in the mood before the show with a little country cookin', call for reservations for the 6 P.M. country dinner. An antique mall is on the property and there's a flea market on weekends.

Wollersheim Winery

7876 Highway 188
Prairie Du Sac
608-643-6515
Type of Activity: Winery tour
Area: About 30 miles from the Dells, Highway 12, left on Highway PF and Highway 60, east to Highway 188, south on 188
Hours: 10 to 5 daily
Cost: $3 for adults, accompanying children 11 and under are free
Author's Rating: ☆☆
Kid Rating: ☆
Teen Rating: ☆
Adult Rating: ☆☆
Senior Rating: ☆☆1/2
Rainy Day Activity: Yes
Comments: Tour this small winery and taste some of Wisconsin's finest wine. Be advised that the winery is a solid 30 minute drive from the Dells area. If you're traveling from the south, one idea is to take Highway 12 as an alternate route (see alternate routes section of this book) and stop at the winery on the way to or from the Dells.

Wonder Spot

Highway 12
608-254-4224
Type of Activity:
Gravity defying attraction
Area: Exit 92, Highway 12
Cost: $4 for adults, $2 for ages 6-12, free for 5 and under
Author's Rating: ☆☆
Kid Rating: ☆☆
Teen Rating: ☆☆
Adult Rating: ☆☆
Senior Rating: ☆
Rainy Day Activity: Yes
Comments: Whether called "Mystery Spot," "Wonder Spot," or something else, this idea is a staple attraction in many tourist towns. If you've never visited a similar attraction, it's worth a visit. The happenings in the Wonder Spot seem to defy gravity. Chairs balance on two legs and people lean over at impossible angles. A wonderfully tacky tourist attraction.

Specialty Activities

Use the following classifications to help you spot activities that might be of particular interest to you. For more information on a particular attraction, refer to the foregoing alphabetical attraction guide.

Golfing

Baraboo Country Club
18 Holes
608-356-8195

Castle Rock Golf Course
Mauston
18 Holes
608-847-4658

Christmas Mountain Village Resort*
Wisconsin Dells
18 Holes
608-254-3971

Coldwater Canyon Golf Course*
Wisconsin Dells
9 Holes
608-254-8489

Devil's Head Resort
Merrimac
18 Holes
608-493-2251

Pinecrest Par 3
Wisconsin Dells
9 Holes – Par 3
608-254-2165

Thal Acres Golf Club
Westfield
18 Holes
608-296-2850

Trapper's Turn Golf Club*
Wisconsin Dells   ˙
18 Holes
608-253-7000

Wilderness Golf Resort*
Wisconsin Dells
18 Holes
608-253-GOLF

*golf course also described
in attractions section

Boat and/or Land Tours

Lower Dells Boat Tour
Mark Twain Boat Tour
The Original Wisconsin Dells Ducks
(Green and White)
Red, White and Blue
(Original WWII) Ducks
Time Travel Geologic
Tours/Nature Safaris
Upper Dells Boat Tour

Mini-Golf

Olde Kilbourn Amusements
Old River
Paul Bunyan's Restaurant
Pirate's Cove
Shipwreck Lagoon
Timber Falls
Western Village
(mini-golf also available
with admission at Noah's Ark)

Water Parks

Family Land
Noah's Ark
Riverview Park & Waterworld

Wildlife Fun

B&H Trout Farm
Beaver Springs Fishing Park
& Riding Stable
Beaver Springs Public Aquarium
Canyon Creek Riding Stable
EZ Rolling Riding Stable
International Crane Foundation
Ranch Riding Stable
Serpent Safari
Time Travel Geologic Tours
and Nature Safaris
Wisconsin Deer Park
Wisconsin Dells Trout Farm

Learning Can Be Fun

H.H. Bennett Studio Foundation
Circus World Museum
Dells Boat Tours
Ducks (either company's tour)
International Crane Foundation
Mid-Continent Railway Museum
Riverside and Great Northern Railway
Preservation Society
Serpent Safari
Stand Rock Indian Ceremonial
Time Travel Tours and Nature Safaris
Tommy Bartlett Robot World
and Exploratory

Unusual and Bizarre
Bill Nehring's Haunted Dungeon
of Horror
Haunted Mansion of Baldazar
Mass Panic
Ripley's Believe It or Not
Serpent Safari
The Wonder Spot
Wax World of the Stars

Fun For The Pre-and-Early-Elementary School Crowd
Lower and Upper Dells Boat Tour
Ducks (either company's tour)
Any of the 3 Water parks
(especially kiddie areas)
Lost Canyon Tours
Storybook Gardens
Tommy Town
Wisconsin Deer Park

For Daredevils
Air Boingo Bungee Jump
Big Chief roller coasters
Adventure Zone Virtual Reality
King Ludwig's Skyscraper
CyberMind Virtual Reality
Extreme World

Wet & Wild Fun
Family Land
Holiday Shores Boat Rental
Lake Delton Water Sports
Noah's Ark
Point Bluff Canoe Rental
Riverview Park & Waterworld
Timber Falls Log Flume Ride

Rainy & Chilly Day Fun
Adventure Zone
H.H. Bennett Photo Studio Museum
Chalet Lanes Bowling
Circus World*
Dells Arcade
Dells Boat Tours*
Dells Ducks (either company's)*
Game Zone

Haunted Mansion of Baldazar
Mid Continent Rail Museum
No Fly Zone
Ripley's Believe It Or Not
Riverside Railroad.Society
Serpent Safari
Tommy Bartlett's Robot World
Tommy Bartlett's Thrill Show*
Wax World of the Stars

* Denotes an attraction that is less
than ideal or may not operate in
very inclement weather

Our Favorite Dells Area Activities:
These are our Dells favorites, listed
in alphabetical order. These are based
solely on our opinion.

Circus World: In season, live
performers provide a true circus
atmosphere

Big Chief: Cool roller coasters
and go-karts

Upper Dells Boat Tours:
A classic Dells experience, and the
boat docks to allow a close up view
of the area's unique geology

Devil's Lake State Park:
Features a breathtaking walking path
that winds up the side of a cliff

International Crane Foundation: Unique, educational and fun

Lost Canyon Tours: Unique,
and short enough to retain maximum
interest

Noah's Ark: The reason why
many people come to the Dells

Original Wisconsin Dells Ducks: A good time for all ages

Ripley's Believe It Or Not:
Weird and wonderful

Tommy Bartlett's Robot World: Hands on and lots of fun

The Wonder Spot: Tacky and
low-rent, but a blast

WATER PARK TOURING TIPS

For many people, water parks are the main Dells attraction. If you don't believe this, drive north on the Parkway just as Noah's Ark is opening for the day. Traffic is backed up considerably.

To enhance your enjoyment of a water park, try these tips:

Look over the park's sales brochure before your visit: All three water parks have brochures with pretty decent maps showing various slides and other important points of interest. Take a few minutes to look over the map, noting the following: (a) what are the park's operating hours on the day of your visit? (b) where are changing rooms, lockers and restrooms? (c) what places could be used as meeting places if people in your group separate over the course of the day? (d) what location would be a convenient "home base"? (e) what slides and rides are of most interest to you and others in your group?

Arrive early and get tickets early if possible: Water park tickets are sometimes available off premises and you can avoid one line by buying tickets before your visit. If you aren't able to do this, simply arrive a few minutes earlier than you might have, had you bought tickets in advance. In any event, get to the park, swimsuit on and ready to slide, at least a few minutes prior to the published opening. Parks are least crowded the first hour after opening and the last hour before closing, and you'll find that during these times, you can slide more in one hour than you can in two or three hours during mid-day. Note that sometimes not all slides are open for the first hour of the park's operation.

Avoid bottlenecks: Try to avoid lines by starting from the back of the park (areas furthest from entrances) and working your way toward entrances. Most people start at the slide nearest to the entrance and work their way toward the back of the park. Also, head for the newest and more popular slides first. Many others will do this as well, but lines will be even longer as the day goes on. Another time to try the most popular slides is in the hour before closing.

Take a midday break: If you are staying nearby, exit the park and head for your motel for a late lunch and rest away from the park. All you'll miss from one to three o'clock is the most crowded period of the day, and you can return refreshed and ready to stay until closing.

Use lockers to your advantage: Parks have a limited number of coin-operated lockers, which are good places for valuables. Most lockers are a little bigger than a foot square, and are located in several places in the park, near changing rooms. If you want a locker, you have to claim one early, as they fill up quickly. Also, make sure you have a supply of quarters to use, and save on quarters by remembering every time you open the locker, you must pay to lock it again.

Claim a chair and set up a "home base": Keep non-valuables (generally speaking, personal belongings are pretty safe, even when unattended for short periods) like food, lotion, towels and the like at a "home base" that everyone in your party knows about. Your group may have a "non-slider" who would like nothing more than to hang out by poolside most of the day—a perfect candidate to occupy the home base chair. If not, put a towel and belongings on the chair and make sure someone stops by now and then to keep it claimed. Once in awhile, someone will remove your stuff and claim the chair, especially if it's unattended for a long time. But, more often than not, your chair will be there and waiting for you or anyone in your party to use.

Keeping track of your party: Since it's easy to get separated, make sure that everyone knows when and where to meet for lunch or at day's end. Clocks are not easy to find at water parks and it's easy to get stuck in a long line, so allow a little flexibility and hope that no one loses track of time too much. Be specific in the meeting place if it's not home base to save time and unnecessary worry. For instance, don't just say, "Let's meet at the Bermuda Triangle." Say, "Let's meet at the exit of Bermuda Triangle."

ONE-DAY TOUR SUGGESTIONS

If you have only one day to spend in the Dells, here are some suggested tour plans, along with approximate costs. For more efficient touring, follow the activities in the order in which they are listed.

The Tots Tour—One-Day Tour With Small Children

This tour is for families with small children. Costs shown are for two adults and two children of admission-paying age. Children five and under are often admitted free, with the exception of Storybook Gardens, which has admission for all children, and Wisconsin Deer Park, which has a charge for children over three years old. A good place to shop for souvenirs for this age group is Parson's Indian Store on the southern portion of Wisconsin Dells Parkway.

Activity	Allow about . . .	Cost
Storybook Gardens	1 to 1-1/2 hours	$ 34
Wisc. Deer Park	1 hour	$ 17
Lunch at Tommy Town	1 hour	$ 12 plus food
Big Chief Go-Karts	up to 1 hour	$ 15
(assume 1 child rides w/adult for free)		
Lower Dells Boat Tour	2 hours	$ 30
Total	6 hours	$ 108

The Terror Tour—One Day Tour With Teens (or Kids Who Think They Are)

This tour is suggested for families with children in the 11-year-old to teens range. Costs assume two adults and two children of 12 and up (adult admissions). Shop for souvenirs in the uptown area.

Activity	Allow about . . .	Cost
Big Chief or King Ludwig's	up to 1 hour	$ 20
(assumes 4 rides/1 per person)		
Mini-Golf at any golf course	1 hour	$ 24 maximum
Virtual Reality ride (uptown)	up to 1 hour	$ 20–25
Lunch uptown	up to 1 hour	$ 20–25
Haunted Mansion/Dungeon	1 hour	$ 24–28
Or Ripleys Believe-It-Or-Not		
Or Serpent Safari		
Ducks Tour (either company)	2 hours	$ 56
Total	6–7 hours	$ 164–$178

Dells-In-A-Day-Till-You-Drop Tour—One Day Tour
For Those With Unlimited Energy and Bottomless Wallets

Ready to arrive early, stay late, move fast, and take out a second mortgage? If so, try this tour. Costs are for four people all paying adult admission. Start at Robot World at 8 A.M. and head over to Noah's Ark upon opening. Enjoy the water park until about noon, then head out for an afternoon of more fun. If you follow the order shown, you'll probably hit the uptown area in the evening hours. Good luck!

Activity	Allow about . . .	Cost
Tommy Bartlett Robot World	1 hour	$ 36
Noah's Ark (bring your suit!)	3–4 hours	$ 80–90
(look for coupons/discounts)		
Big Chief or King Ludwig's	up to 1 hour	$ 20
(assumes 4 rides/1 per person)		
Mini-Golf at any golf course	1 hour	$ 24 maximum
Lunch	up to 1 hour	$ 20–25
Serpent Safari	1 hour	$ 28
Wonder Spot	1 hour	$ 16
Virtual Reality ride (uptown)	up to 1 hour	$ 20–25
Haunted Mansion/Dungeon	1 hour	$ 28
Or Ripley's Believe-It-Or-Not		
Ducks Tour (either company)	2 hours	$ 56
Total	12–14 hours	$ 328–$348

DINING IN THE DELLS

Eating in the Dells area can easily turn from an enjoyable experience to an unpleasant inconvenience, depending on the season, time of day, and your location. Often, the biggest challenge is getting to a restaurant, which during busy season often means fighting traffic or a long walk. When you arrive at the restaurant, if it's during peak days and times, it will likely be quite crowded, and you will face a sizeable wait, since few restaurants take reservations. What can you do to beat the crowds? Here are some ideas:

1. Many lodging places offer an in-room refrigerator, microwave oven, and coffee maker. You may wish to bring food for at least breakfast and lunch, and eat in your room or in your motel's picnic area. If you should go this route, refer to the menu and shopping list below.

   ### Breakfast menu ideas
   Bagels and cream cheese
   Cold cereal and milk
   Fresh fruit
   Sweet rolls or donuts
   Canned/bottled juice

   ### Lunch ideas
   Cold meat sandwiches
   Chips
   Fresh veggies with dip
   Fresh fruit
   Soft drinks

   ### Shopping List:
   Paper plates
   Plastic utensils
   Bowls for cereal
   Paper towels
   Napkins
   Disposable cups

   Note on food items:
   for sandwiches,
   don't forget butter, mayo,
   mustard, catsup, etc.

2. If you choose to eat only one meal out, you can dodge the dinner crowd by eating out at lunch time and have a lighter meal in the evening.
3. If you want to eat out during the evening rush period, beat the crowds by going earlier or later than the majority of diners. Least crowded is the 4 to 5 P.M. period, but for fast-food and family-oriented places, after 7 P.M. is sometimes less crowded as well.
4. Order out for delivery. Many pizza places and other restaurants deliver to motels. Some restaurants deliver via a service, which can be reached by calling 253-DINE. There is a $10 minimum order plus a service charge. Delivery hours are 4 to 11:30 P.M.
5. Send one brave soul from your party out to pick up food. There are several places that are geared to carry-out service, especially in the uptown area.

Restaurants

Our Restaurant Favorites

The Dells has something for everyone when it comes to food. If you want fast food, it's easy to find (with the possible exception of some parts of the Parkway). Sit-down family restaurants abound. Want Italian? Pizza? Steak? Burgers? A buffet? Most of these have a dozen restaurants competing for your food dollar. Want *really good* food and *fast, friendly* service? Well…that can be a little tougher to come by, especially in the busy months. That said, here are some suggestions for a better-than-average food experience.

In the fast-food category let's start uptown. The **Shrimp Shack** has to be one of the more unique fast-food menus, specializing in – you guessed it – carry-out shrimp, as well as other seafood. **Culver's** is a Wisconsin-based chain with (in our opinion) the best burgers and frozen custard in the area, if not in the world. **Dick's Dough** makes a great funnel cake to eat on the go, and makes a great dessert to follow a hot dog from **Teenies**. Away from the Broadway area, most fast-food choices are the national chains. The **Burger King** on Highway 13 (exit 87 area) is huge, and has a nice play area. The **Subway** on the Parkway is clean and has a small, but decent sized seating area. **Jimmy's Hot Dogs** on the Parkway serves a nice Chicago-style hot dog, and right around the corner on Highway 12, **Mary's Place** is another hot dog/burger choice. If pizza is your favorite, **Rocky Rococo's** on Stand Rock Road has wonderful pan style pizza by the slice or whole pie.

For family-style restaurants, there are plenty of good choices. **Henny Penny** on the Parkway is a solid bet. Further up the Parkway, **Mr. Pancake** is a good IHOP-style restaurant. Uptown, the **Family Chef** and the **Park Restaurant** are good choices. We also like **Denny's Diner** on the corner of Dells Parkway and Munroe Street in Lake Delton. **Upper Crust** on Broadway has a nice pizza/pasta menu. If you want to see a real-life, old-time restaurant that doesn't have to pretend to be nostalgic, check out the **Dells Grill** on Broadway.

If you want to relax with a beer or drink with your meal, in the Parkway area we suggest **Houlihan's** or **The Embers**. Houlihan's has a less formal menu, while Embers leans more toward a supper club atmosphere. Nearby, **Ravina Bay** just off the Parkway is a good choice. Uptown, we suggest **Monks Bar & Grill**, **The Sand Bar**, and the **Country Keg** saloon. In other areas, **Field's Steak and Stein** is a great place, as is the **Mesa Grill** in the Chula Vista Resort and the **Wintergreen Grill** in the Wintergreen Resort. **The Pizza Pub** (Dells Parkway) and **Pumphouse Pizza** (Munroe Street) are probably the most hopping pizza places in the area.

Buffets are abundant in the Dells. **Paul Bunyan** is one of the originals, and offers a breakfast buffet in the morning as well as other meals later in the day. Right across the road, **Black Bart's** serves breakfast and dinner buffets. At Black Bart's, kids are charged according to their height. The **Polish-American Buffet** at the American Club on the Parkway is an interesting choice. Also on the Parkway, a good bet is the **Big Country Buffet**.

Restaurants by Area

Key: A "C" denotes that the restaurant either has limited or no seating, or that it specializes in carryout food. Well-known fast-food chains obviously offer carryout, so are not marked as such. An "S" indicates a restaurant that actively promotes delivery service. Please note that some other restaurants may also offer carryout and/or delivery, but do not actively promote it.

Wisconsin Dells Parkway from South End to North End:

Country Supermarket (grocery and deli)—near south end of Parkway—C

Jimmy's Hotdogs—126 Wisconsin Dells Parkway—C: Chicago-style hotdogs

Subway—421 Wisconsin Dells Parkway—C—nice version of chain, with some seating

Ravina Bay Restaurant—a few blocks off the Parkway on Lake Delton—bar/restaurant atmosphere

Delton Food Shoppe—524 Wisconsin Dells Parkway—C—convenience store

Houlihans—644 Wisconsin Dells Parkway—family oriented grill & bar

Del Bar—800 Wisconsin Dells Parkway—bar/grill/supper club

House of Embers—935 Wisconsin Dells Parkway—supper club with strong following

Henny Penny—1010 Wisconsin Dells Parkway—sandwiches, home-made fare

BJs Restaurant—Wisconsin Dells Parkway across from Flamingo—burgers, pizza and the like—also breakfast

Mr. Pancake—1405 Wisconsin Dells Parkway—waffles, omelets, and—yes—pancakes

Dairy Queen—1500 Wisconsin Dells Parkway—one of two local entries of national chain

Pizza Pub—1455 Wisconsin Dells Parkway—CD—pizza, salad bar, Italian food, bar adjacent

Tommy Town—1470 Wisconsin Dells Parkway—fast-food (pizza) with large pay-to-play area

Brothers in Law—1481 Wisconsin Dells Parkway—bar, outdoor beer garden

Big Country Buffet—1531 Wisconsin Dells Parkway—one of many buffets in area

Bomberino's—1810 Wisconsin Dells Parkway—Italian-oriented buffet

Lighthouse Pizza—196 State Highway 13—in Dells boat dock complex

Polish American Buffet/American Club—intersection 400 County Highway A & Wisconsin Dells Parkway—the name says it all

Kountry Kousin—Wisconsin Dells Parkway—another buffet entry

Howie's Restaurant—Wisconsin Dells Parkway—specializes in breakfast, but serves other meals too

The Root Beer Stand—Wisconsin Dells Parkway & Highway 13—C—drive-up, carry-out specialties

Country Kitchen—State Highway 12—part of regional chain of family restaurants, breakfast & sandwiches are specialties

Exit 87, From Exit to the Dells Parkway intersection:

Perkins—811 North Frontage Road—local representative of national chain

Burger King—Highway 13 at County Highway H

Wendy's—630 South Frontage Road

Black Bart's Stagecoach Buffet—State Highway 13—theme buffet for breakfast and dinner

Paul Bunyan's—State Highway 13—one of the better known buffets in the area

Denny's—600 South Frontage Road

Taco Bell—State Highway 13

From Wisconsin Dells Parkway through uptown Dells:

Rocky Rococo Pizza—1012 Stand Rock Road—CD—pan-style pizza by the slice or pie, salad bar

Pedro's Mexican—951 Stand Rock Road—area chain, Mexican food sit-down restaurant

Wok Works—1051 Stand Rock Road—CD—fast food, carryout emphasis

Bean Berry Bistro Gourmet Food & Drink—1021 Stand Rock Road—CD—gourmet selections at reasonable prices

Showboat—24 Broadway—bar/restaurant atmosphere

Chester Fried Chicken—Broadway—C—fast-food chicken

The Sand Bar (bar & grill)—744 Eddy St.—bar and grill

Nig's (bar & grill)—201 Broadway—more bar than grill

Fabulous Frozen Yogurt—on River Road just off Broadway—C

Monks Bar & Grill—220 Broadway—CD—bar with good food selection

Upper Crust—232 Broadway—Italian specialties, pizza, located upstairs

Teenies—on Superior St. just off Broadway—C—carry-out hotdogs, gyros, and sandwiches

Pizza Villa Italian Café—on Superior St. just off Broadway—Italian specialties

Dairy Queen—Broadway—C—uptown entry of local chain, carry-out

Subway—Broadway—C

Roeker's Bakery—Broadway—C—local bakery

Culvers—312 Broadway—C—area chain with burgers and frozen custard

Broadway Bar & Grill—324 Broadway

Steak Haus on Broadway—Broadway & Oak—very casual

King Louis XV Café—221 Broadway—C—hot dogs and the like

O'Conners—Broadway—bar and grill atmosphere

Dell Haus—Broadway

Country Keg Saloon—713 Oak St.—bar and grill atmosphere

The Shrimp Shack—741 Oak St., just off Broadway—CD—carryout, fast-food-style shrimp and seafood

Dick's Dough—Broadway—C—
funnel cakes and ice cream are the
house specialties
Dells Grill—Broadway—an actual
traditional diner complete with
counter seating
Hole in the Wall Bar & Restaurant—
Broadway—bar, restaurant,
weekend live entertainment
Western Village shops and eateries—
C—includes a couple of fast-food,
carry-out places
Fitzgerald's—Broadway—family-
oriented restaurant adjacent to
motel
Park Restaurant—701 Broadway—
family-oriented
Family Chef—1101 Broadway—also
family-oriented

Exit 92 to Wisconsin Dells Parkway (Lake Delton):

Annie's Italian Port—S1675 Ishnala
Road—Italian specialties
McDonalds–U.S. Highway 12 near
I-90/94 exit
Subway—U.S. Highway 12 near
I-90/94 exit
Danny's Diner—U.S. Highway 12
near I-90/94 exit—C—burgers, etc.
in modern version of diner
Ponderosa—940 U.S. Highway 12—
national chain
Wintergreen Grill—behind
McDonald's off Highway 12—
pizza buffet is a specialty
Bar-B-Q Bills—U.S. Highway 12—
barbecue, outdoor seating
Cheese Factory—521 U.S. Highway
12—C—cheese and vegetarian
specialties
Mary's Place—133 U.S. Highway
12—C—hot dogs and burgers
Fischer's Supper Club—U.S. Highway
12—supper club menu

KFC—31 U.S. Highway 12 (near
intersection with Wisconsin Dells
Parkway North)

Exit 89 to Wisconsin Dells Parkway

Pumphouse Pizza—19 West Munroe
(near intersection with Wisconsin
Dells Parkway North)—CD—also
features microbrewery
Not Just Bagels—11 West Munroe
(near intersection with Wisconsin
Dells Parkway North)—C—bakery
Denny's Diner—Corner of 12
(Wisconsin Dells Parkway) &
Munroe—old-style diner known for
its cinnamon rolls
Bake Shop—Munroe Street—bakery
items

Other Areas:

Mulligan's—Christmas Mountain
Village
Ishnala Supper Club—Lake Delton—
short drive from Exit 92 area
Mesa Grill & Luigi's Pizza—Chula
Vista Resort, Highway 13 exit 87
area
Port Vista—1280 E Hiawatha
Stuffs Sandwiches—State Highway
13, look for the yellow car out front
Field's Steak and Stein—State
Highway 13, near Chula Vista
Resort
Otto's Supper Club—just south of
Wisconsin Dells on State
Highway 16

Restaurants by Type

Convenience/Grocery/Deli:
Country Supermarket
Delton Food Shop
Uptown Bakery
Not Just Bagels

Fast Food:

Jimmy's Hotdogs
Subway (Wisconsin Dells Parkway &
    Exit 92 areas & Uptown)
Dairy Queen
Tommy Town
The Root Beer Stand
Burger King
Wendy's
Taco Bell
Rocky Roccoco Pizza
Bean Berry Bistro
    (also other selections)
Culver's
The Shrimp Shack
Teenies
Dick's Dough
King Louis XV
Cactus Cafe
Bake Shop
McDonald's
Danny's Diner
Fabulous Frozen Yogurt
KFC
Wok Works
Stuffs Sandwiches

**Sit-down—Family (table service,
no alcohol served):**

Henny Penny
BJ's Restaurant
Howie's
Mr. Pancake
Country Kitchen
Dell Haus
Perkins
Denny's
Denny's Diner
Family Chef
Cheese Factory
Ponderosa Steak House
Paul Bunyan's
Park Restaurant
Steak Haus on Broadway

**Sit-down—Casual (table service,
alcohol served):**

Ravina Bay Restaurant
Houlihans
Pizza Pub
Lighthouse
Pedro's Mexican
Showboat
The Sand Bar
Hole in the Wall Bar & Restaurant
Nig's Bar & Grill
Monk's Bar & Grill (also carryout and
    delivery)
Pizza Villa Italian Cafe
The Spare Room Sports Bar and Grill
Country Keg Saloon
Pizza Pub
Broadway Bar & Grill
Pumphouse Pizza
Wintergreen Grill
Mulligans at Christmas Mountain
    Village
Field's Steak and Stein

**Sit-down—Supperclub
atmosphere (table service,
alcohol served, more formal
menu choices):**

Del Bar
House of Embers
Fischer's Supper Club
Otto's Supper Club

**Buffet: (note: other restaurants
may also offer buffets at various
times)**

Big Country Buffet
Black Bart's Stagecoach Buffet
Kountry Kousin
American Club/Polish American
    Buffet
Wintergreen Grill (Pizza Buffet, also
    other menu items)

SHOPPING

Shops in the Dells area cover a wide range of products. There are certainly enough T-shirt shops in the Uptown area alone to satisfy the demands of any tourist. But there are many other shopping options to choose from. A more thorough listing is at the end of this section, but here are some highlights of what we feel are the most interesting stores.

Antiques

Our favorite antique-shopping area is Oak Street, located just off Broadway. Here you'll find three antique shops: Antique Mall of Wisconsin Dells, Days Gone By, and Oak Street Antiques. The largest and most interesting product selection is probably at the **Antique Mall of Wisconsin Dells**. This large store has a particular emphasis on toys and autographed sports memorabilia, but has a large selection of just about everything else, too. **Days Gone By Antique Mall's** strong suit is printed material—they have a particularly strong selection of books, comics, posters, postcards, and trading cards, as well as other items. Be sure to check out the book room upstairs. **Oak Street Antiques** has a nice selection, but its most unique area is called **Jan's Barbie Emporium**. In the Lake Delton area, check out **Old Academy**, located on U.S. Highway 12 in an old church building.

Arts and Crafts Galleries

In the immediate Dells area, there aren't many true arts and crafts galleries. There are a number of them in Baraboo, about 20 minutes away. In Wisconsin Dells itself, **the Loonery** offers the best choice. It is a huge store, divided into several theme "shops," such as bird houses, wood carvings, glassware, and so forth. The Loonery is located just off Broadway on Oak Street near the antique malls.

Candy

While candy shops are not as ubiquitous as gift stores, there are more than enough to challenge any dieter. Our very favorite is actually on U.S. Highway 12 toward Baraboo. Just a little way past Ho-Chunk Casino is the **Baraboo Candy Company**, an outlet store of sorts. Here you'll find the Cowpie candy bar, a wonderful mixture of chocolate, caramel, and nuts that is shaped in a patty. The store also carries many other candies, including a wide choice of sugar-free selections. On Broadway, don't miss a chance to eat some of the best fudge anywhere. Our favorites are **Grandma's Fudge**, **Swiss Maid Fudge**, and **Wisconsin Dairyland Fudge**. All have tasty fudge made right in the store, and other homemade candy as well. Finally,

Goody Goody Gumdrop Company has stores on Dells Parkway (near Waterworld) and on Broadway.

Gifts and Souvenirs

When it comes to gift shops in the Dells, we're tempted to try this experiment: Anywhere in the Dells, but especially on Broadway, close your eyes and toss a dime. We think there's a strong chance you'll hit a gift shop, probably one that sells T-shirts or moccasins. Our favorites for Dells gifts include Parson's Indian Trading Post, Tradewinds, Aunt Jenny's Got It All, Glass Unicorne, Holiday House, and Native Sun Gifts. **Parson's Indian Trading Post** (south end of Wisconsin Dells Parkway) is a huge store which carries a great selection of clothing, toys, handcrafted items, moccasins, and hats. They also have a nice arts-and-crafts section where you can buy beads and supplies. Prices are pretty reasonable by Dells standards. The strong suit of **Tradewinds** (Broadway) is a unique selection of sculpture, mobiles, and wind chimes made from seashells. **Aunt Jenny's Got It All** (adjacent to Pirate's Cove Golf) certainly lives up to its name with a broad selection of everything a tourist could think of. **Glass Unicorne** (Broadway) specializes in high-end glass items including stained glass, figurines, and hand-blown glass. **Native Sun Gifts** (Broadway) carries some interesting Native American-theme products. We like **Holiday House** (Broadway) because it has a certain quiet atmosphere that rises above the tourist-hustle-and-bustle feeling of other shops.

T-Shirts and Clothing

Broadway's name could be changed to "T-shirt Street" to more accurately describe it. There are countless stores selling clothing, with T-shirts the featured item in most of them. For swimwear, the **Splish Splash Shops** (Broadway and south end of Dells Parkway) have a nice selection of swimwear and accessories. **Vacation Station** (where U.S. Highway 12 turns north to become Wisconsin Dells Parkway) is also a good place to stop on the way to the water park if you forgot anything. **Too Cute**, located on Broadway, has a pretty wide selection of swimwear for women. A good off-Broadway choice is **Sun Gear,** which is actually part of a cluster of connected shops located next to Serpent Safari on Wisconsin Dells Parkway. If name-brand athletic wear and licensed wear (Green Bay Packers wear, especially) is your thing, don't miss **Sports Impressions,** located just off Broadway on Superior Street. The same advice applies to shopping for moccasins, although you may also want to pay a visit to **Parson's Indian Trading Post** if you're looking for mocs or hats. For T-shirts, it's beyond our mental capacity (and probably the capacity of the world's largest supercomputer) to sort through the choices. The best advice is to take a walk around the Uptown area for the shirt store that best suits your tastes.

USEFUL ADDRESSES AND PHONE NUMBERS

Where Can I Find...?

Antiques

Antique Mall of Wisconsin Dells
720 Oak Street
Wisc. Dells
608-254-2422

Braun's Happy Landings Antiques
30 N Jetson St.
Lake Delton
608-253-4613

Days Gone By Antique Mall
729-731 Oak Street
Wisc. Dells

608-254-6788
Oak Street Antiques
725 Oak Street
Wisc. Dells
608-254-4200

Old Academy Antiques and Gifts Mall
Highway 12
Lake Delton
608-254-4948

Our Gang Antique Mall
Highway 23
Lake Delton
608-254-4401

Rich's Antiques
133 3rd Avenue
Baraboo
608-356-0844

Risley Brothers Emporium
129 3rd Street
Baraboo
608-355-1090

Art Galleries

Cornerstone Gallery
101 4th St.
Baraboo
608-356-7805

Elephant's Tear Gallery
532 Oak St.
Baraboo
608-356-5650

Frameworks and Wildlife Gallery
2275 E Main St.
Reedsburg
800-467-2333

Main Street Art
151 Main St.
Reedsburg
608-524-1327

Shadow Box Gallery
S5077 Lovers Lane
Baraboo
608-356-5005

Auto Rental

Avis Rent-a-Car
Highway 13
Wisc. Dells
608-254-7773

Country Corner Rental
Highway 12 & 33
Baraboo
608-356-2181

Enterprise Rent-a-Car
630 Highway 12
Baraboo
608-355-7600

Glacier Valley Ford
615 South Blvd
Baraboo
608-356-2222

Kruse Oldsmobile
515 Broadway
Baraboo
608-356-4919

Automobile Repair Shops (Wisconsin Dells and Lake Delton Only)

Broadway Mobil
802 Broadway
Wisc. Dells
608-254-7623

Dells Auto Center
S75 Highway A
Wisc. Dells
608-254-7199

Dick Reiter Chevrolet-Buick-Geo
W15210 Highway 16
Wisc. Dells
608-253-1191

Hitchcock's Service Center
Highway 12 and I-90/94
Lake Delton
608-254-6198

Outback Auto
W1704 Smith Road
Wisc. Dells
608-254-6375

Rodwell, Jim
22 Whitlock St
Wisc. Dells
608-253-6188

TEC Auto Body
N549 Highways 12 & 16
Wisc. Dells
608-254-2296

Bakeries

Bakers Dozen Bakery
424 Oak St.
Baraboo
608-356-2995

Gardner Baking Co
401 Linn St
Baraboo
608-356-4743

Roeker's Bakery
228 Broadway
Wisc. Dells
608-253-4351

Banks (Wisconsin Dells and Lake Delton Only)

Bank of Wisconsin Dells
716 Superior St.
Wisc. Dells
608-253-1111

Bank of Mauston–Dells Delton Branch
402 County Road A
Wisc. Dells
608-253-7030

M&I Mid-State Bank
501 Washington Ave.
Wisc. Dells
608-254-2513

Barbers

The Hair Center
718 Oak St.
Wisc. Dells
608-254-7720

The Kut Hut
606 Oak St.
Baraboo
608-356-6646

Mike's Barber Shop
116 3rd St.
Baraboo
608-356-6590

Sam's Barber Shop
410 Oak St.
Baraboo
608-356-3737

Beauty Salons

Anna's Country Cuts
5310 Highway 113
Baraboo
608-356-4392

Cher-Laines Hair Affair
507 South Blvd.
Baraboo
608-356-4885

Cinder-Fellas Hair Salon
233 4th St.
Baraboo
608-356-4233

The Clip Joint
Highway 23
Lake Delton
608-254-8775

Co-ed Classics
324-1/2 Wisconsin Ave.
Wisc. Dells
608-254-7373

Cost Cutters
623 Westdayl Plaza
Baraboo
608-356-1004

Cut Above Hair Center
3961 Co. Road G
Wisc. Dells
608-253-3771

Golden Shears Styling Studio
1211 8th St.
Baraboo
608-356-2000

Hair Care
636 7th Ave.
Baraboo
608-356-7055

Hair & Nail Spa Plus
102 4th Ave.
Baraboo
608-356-1155

Hair Unlimited
601 Washington Ave.
Baraboo
608-356-1118

Haircut Express
912 8th Ave.
Baraboo
608-356-4997

Hairloom
720 Lincoln Ave.
Baraboo
608-356-7654

Lisa Hohl
112 4th Ave.
Baraboo
608-355-7547

LaPetite Beauty & Tanning
1025 Elm St.
Wisc. Dells
608-254-2581

Looking Good
924 8th Ave.
Baraboo
608-356-5250

New Image Hair Designs
702 Oak St.
Baraboo
608-356-5600

PS Cuts
305 Broadway
Wisc. Dells
608-254-2328

Shear Class
618 Oak St.
Baraboo
608-356-1840

TJ's Hairazors
405 Willow St.
Baraboo
608-356-6013

Total Design Salon
112 4th Ave.
Baraboo
608-356-6151

Car Washes
Automit Car Wash
1015 8th St.
Baraboo
608-356-8665

Clean Concepts
101 N Grasser Rd.
Lake Delton
608-253-5078

Viking Express Store & Car Wash
1375 E Main St.
Baraboo
608-356-6969

Wonder Wash
1120 Jefferson St.
Baraboo
608-356-8517

Churches
(denomination in parentheses)
Baraboo Assembly of God Church
(Assembly of God)
1000 11th St.
Baraboo
608-356-8977

Keystone Baptist Church (Baptist)
E10003A Trout Rd.
Wisc. Dells
608-254-2063

Walnut Hills Bible Church (Baptist)
1900 East St
Baraboo
608-356-3111

St. Cecelia's Church (Catholic)
604 Oak St.
Wisc. Dells
608-254-8381

St. Joseph's Catholic Church
(Catholic)
304 East St.
Baraboo
608-356-4773

Christian Science Reading Room
(Christian Science)
602 East St.
Baraboo
608-356-3801

Church of Christ (Church of God)
150 Shaw Road W
Baraboo
608-356-6545

Church of Jesus Christ of Latter-day
Saints (Mormon)
813 Iroquois Circle
Baraboo
608-356-2052

Holy Cross Church (Episcopal)
322 Unity Dr.
Wisc. Dells
608-254-8623

Trinity Episcopal Church (Episcopal)
111 6th St.
Baraboo
608-356-3620

Kingdom Hall (Jehovah's Witness)
Hatchery Road
Baraboo
608-356-4288

Our Savior Lutheran Church
(Lutheran)
1120 Draper St.
Baraboo
608-356-9792

St. John's Lutheran Church (Lutheran)
624 East St.
Baraboo
608-355-3870

Trinity Lutheran Church (Lutheran)
728 Church St.
Wisc. Dells
608-253-3241

Bethany Evangelical Lutheran Church (Lutheran)
620 E Broadway
Wisc. Dells
608-254-4501

St. Paul's Evangelical Lutheran Church (Lutheran)
727 8th St.
Baraboo
608-356-3230

Emanuel Church (United Methodist)
101 14th St.
Baraboo
608-356-8246

First United Methodist Church (United Methodist)
615 Broadway
Baraboo
608-356-3991

United Methodist Church
of Dells Delton (United Methodist)
320 Unity Dr.
Wisc. Dells
608-253-6511

Church of the Nazarene (Nazarene)
1800 Crawford St.
Baraboo
608-356-3774

Living Hope Church
(non-denominational)
S3963 Highway 12
Baraboo
608-356-7979

United Presbyterian Church (Presbyterian)
730 Cedar St.
Wisc. Dells
608-253-3481

First Presbyterian Church (Presbyterian USA)
416 Ash St.
Baraboo
608-356-5945

First Congregational Church (United Church of Christ)
131 6th Ave.
Baraboo
608-356-4300

Parkway Wesleyan Church (Weslayen)
330 Parkway St.
Baraboo
608-356-8112

Cleaners, Laundries and Self-service Laundries

Badger Cleaners
616 Oak St.
Baraboo
608-356-5210

Circus City One-Hour Cleaners
721 Broadway
Baraboo
608-356-4441

Coachlight Laundromat
717 Broadway
Baraboo
608-356-7448

Lake Dells Cleaners
741 Elm St.
Wisc. Dells
608-254-6227

Top-2-Bottom Cleaners
713 DuBois Dr. W
Baraboo
608-356-7701

Wisconsin Dells Laundromat
741 Elm St.
Wisc. Dells
608-254-6227

DJT Linen Service
S1173 Birchwood Road
Wisc. Dells
608-253-7130

Parkside Laundromat
802 Broadway
Wisc. Dells
608-254-7805

Quick Service Laundry
614 Michigan Ave
Wisc. Dells
608-254-8732

Clinics—Medical
Dells Clinic
1310 Broadway
Wisc. Dells
608-253-1171/356-2814

Medical Associates of Baraboo
1700 Tuttle
Baraboo
608-355-3800

Contact Lenses
Forsythe & Forsythe Optometrists
526 Vine St.
Wisc. Dells
608-254-8383

Midwest Vision Centers
144 4th Ave.
Baraboo
608-356-3610

Convenience Stores
(most have gasoline)
Casey's General Store
801 Boulevard
Baraboo
608-356-6735

The Corner Pump
3303 State Highway 13
Wisc. Dells
608-254-4546

Dan's Amoco
Highway 12
Wisc. Dells
608-254-7988

Delton Food Shoppe
524 Wisc. Dells Parkway
Wisc. Dells
608-254-4000

Dino Stop
421 Wisc. Dells Parkway
Wisc. Dells
608-254-8577

Eve's Country Store
3716 State Road 13
Wisc. Dells
608-254-7838

Hovie's Mountain Trading Post
Highway H
Wisc. Dells
608-254-3963

Lake Delton Mobil Travel Mart
1171 Wisc. Dells Parkway
Wisc. Dells
608-254-7810

Lower Dells Mobil
710 Trout Rd.
Wisc. Dells
608-254-8523

M&G Travel Mart
617 W Pine
Baraboo
608-356-1067
110 Wisc. Dells Parkway
Lake Delton
608-254-7444

One Stop
1425-1 Wisc. Dells Parkway
Lake Delton
608-253-7867

Terri's Short Stop
152 Munroe St.
Lake Delton
608-254-6947

Turner's Water Store & Self Serve
413 Highway 12
Baraboo
608-356-1144

Uncle Dan's Stop & Shop
911 Highway 12
Wisc. Dells
608-254-4488

Viking Express Store & Car Wash
1375 E Main St
Baraboo
608-356-6969

Dentists
Baxter Dental Center
880 14th St.
W. Baraboo
608-356-3838

Robert Carlson, DDS
805 River Road
Wisc. Dells
608-254-2345

Dental Associates of Baraboo
880 14th St.
Baraboo
608-356-6611

Thomas Hatch, DDS
320 Race St.
Wisc. Dells
608-254-6830

Robert Konen
314 Ash St.
Baraboo
608-356-3790

Monte McFadden, DDS
1030 8th St.
Baraboo
608-356-4141

Patrick Sweeney, DDS
910 Iowa Ave.
Wisc. Dells
608-253-4701

Department Stores
K-Mart Store
619 Highway 136
Baraboo
608-356-7835

Wal-Mart Store
315 W. Pine St.
Baraboo
608-356-1765

Fire Departments
Emergencies Only—Dial 911

Fishing—Bait
Annie's Bait Shop
137 Linn St.
W. Baraboo
608-356-6294

B&H Trout Farm
3640 State Road 13
Wisc. Dells
608-254-7280

River's Edge Bait Shop
Highway A
Wisc. Dells
608-254-6494

Schleef's Bait Shop
1141 E. Hiawatha
Wisc. Dells
608-254-2034

Viking Express Conv. Store
818 8th St.
Baraboo
608-356-6969

Gifts and Souvenirs (includes sportswear)

Adams Street Gift Shop
41 Adams St.
Lake Delton

Arnold Borcher Company
216 Broadway
Wisc. Dells
608-254-8386

Aunt Jenny's Got It All
Highway 12
Wisc. Dells
608-254-2565

Bailey's Landing
131 Broadway
Wisc. Dells
608-254-8721

The Blue Parrot
741 Superior St.
Wisc. Dells
608-254-7293

Broadway Bargains
Broadway
Wisc. Dells

Chalet Shops
232 Broadway
(upstairs from Chalet Bowling)
Includes: Gift Gallery, The RACES,
Sandee's Treasures, Poor Ole Patti's,
and Christmas Dreams
608-254-8386

Creative Energies
127 4th St.
Baraboo
608-355-0110

Dells Outlet Store
405 Broadway
Wisc. Dells
608-253-7343

Downie's Home Sweet Home
840 Highway 12
Baraboo
608-356-4444

Gift House Christmas World
130 4th Ave.
Baraboo
608-356-5446

Gifts of the World
923 Wisc. Dells Parkway
Lake Delton
608-253-5261

The Glass Unicorne
Broadway
Wisc. Dells

Golden Eagle Sportwear
320 Broadway
Wisc. Dells
608-254-2074

Hills Gallery & Gifts
121 4th St.
Baraboo
608-356-8383

Holiday House
329 Broadway
Wisc. Dells
608-254-8672

Jerry's Gifts and Collectibles
516 Oak St.
Baraboo
608-356-6901

Just Imagine/Not Just Toys
120 4th Ave.
Baraboo
608-356-5507

The Loonery Arts & Crafts
714 Oak St.
Wisc. Dells
608-253-7131

The Moccasin Shop
122 Broadway
Wisc. Dells
608-253-4641

The Music Box
Superior St.
Wisc. Dells

Native Sun Resort Wear & Gifts
302 Broadway
Wisc. Dells
608-253-6584

Nautical Notions
117 3rd St.
Baraboo
608-356-8511

Parson's Indian Trading Post
370 Wisconsin Dells Parkway
Lake Delton
608-254-8533

Paul Bunyan's Restaurant & Gifts
411 Highway 13
Wisc. Dells
608-254-8717

Raining Cats and Dogs
830 Highway 12
Baraboo
608-356-1101

The Robot Connection Gift Shop
(Tommy Bartlett's Robot World)
510 Wisc. Dells Parkway
Lake Delton
608-254-7560
Also location on Broadway

Scent-Sations
Broadway
Wisc. Dells

Shells
Superior St.
Wisc. Dells

Special Affects
1000 Stand Rock Road
Wisc. Dells
608-253-7923

Splish Splash Beach Store
326 Broadway
Wisc. Dells
608-253-7848

Sports Impressions
731 Superior St.
Wisc. Dells
608-254-4919

Subway Center Gifts
421 Wisc. Dells Parkway
Wisc. Dells
608-253-9277

Summer Scene
Broadway
Wisc. Dells

Sun Gear
1425 Wisc. Dells Parkway
Wisc. Dells
608-254-4097

Thirty-Eight (38) Broadway
38 Broadway
Wisc. Dells
608-254-4101

The Teepee
118 Broadway
Wisc. Dells
608-254-2456

Too Cute
214 Broadway
Wisc. Dells
608-253-9051

The Uptown Shop
305 Broadway
Wisc. Dells
608-254-7020

Uptown Trading Post
305 Broadway
Wisc. Dells
608-254-8733

View of the Dells Gifts
Hwys. 12, 13, 16 & 23
Wisc. Dells
608-254-8336

Wild Apples
302 8th St.
Baraboo
608-356-1009

Wild Bird Barn
830 Highway 12
Baraboo
608-356-2920

Winnebago Gift Shop
226 Broadway
Wisc. Dells
608-254-2616

Grocery Stores
(also see Convenience Stores)
C & H Supermarket
732 Oak St.
Wisc. Dells
608-254-7919

Country Market
Wisc. Dells Parkway
Lake Delton
608-254-8348

Darrow's Country Market
1212 8th St.
Baraboo
608-356-2106

Pierce's Pick 'n Save
615 Highway 136
Baraboo
608-356-6671

Zinke's Shop Rite and Liquor Store
216 Washington Ave
Wisc. Dells
608-254-8313

Hardware Stores
Co-op Country Partners
935 8th St.
Baraboo
608-356-2721

Isenberg's True Value Hardware
1220 8th St.
Baraboo
608-356-8785

Steffe's True Value Hardware
310 Broadway
Wisc. Dells
608-253-2201

Hospitals/Emergency Rooms

Adams County Memorial Hospital
402 W Lake St.
Friendship
608-339-3331

Devine Savior Hospital
1015 W Pleasant St.
Portage
608-742-4131

Hess Memorial Hospital/
Mile Bluff Medical Center
1050 Division St.
Mauston
608-847-6161

Reedsburg Area Medical Center
2000 N Dewey Ave
Reedsburg
608-524-6487

St. Clare Hospital
707 14th St.
Baraboo
608-356-5561

Liquor Stores

American World Liquor Store
400 Cty A and WDP
Wisc. Dells
608-253-4451

Mr. K's Bottle Shop
Hwy. 12—WDP South
Lake Delton
608-254-7646

Stoppin Point Liquors
433 Linn St.
Baraboo
608-356-8220

Pharmacies

Broadway Travel Mart
802 Broadway
Wisc. Dells
608-253-4231

Corner Drug Store
522 Oak St.
Baraboo
608-356-8701

Lombard's Clinic Pharmacy
1700 Tuttle St.
Baraboo
608-356-6966

Police and Sheriff Departments

Emergencies Only—911

Lake Delton
608-254-8331 (non-emergency)

Wisconsin Dells
608-253-1611 (non-emergency)

Columbia County Sheriff
608-742-4166

Sauk County Sheriff
608-356-4895

Sporting Goods

Baraboo Surplus Plus
111 2nd St.
Baraboo
608-356-7342

Devil's Lake Camp Store
S5975 Park Road
Baraboo
608-356-7781

Sport Haven
Highway 12 & 33
W. Baraboo
608-356-9218

Steffe's True Value Hardware
310 Broadway
Wisc. Dells
608-253-2201

Wheeler's Campground
E11329 Highway 159
Baraboo
608-356-4877

Veterinarians
Baraboo Valley Clinic
403 South Parkway
Baraboo
608-355-2882

Dells Animal Hospital
4135 Highway 13   Wisc. Dells
253-7361

Video Rentals
Movie Gallery
717 Broadway
Baraboo
608-356-0253

Showtime Video
812 Church St.
Wisc. Dells
608-253-7469

Showtime Video
421 Wisc. Dells Pkwy
Lake Delton
608-254-7469

Viking Express Conv. Store
818 8th St.
Baraboo
608-356-6969

INDEX

READER INPUT SURVEY

Dear Reader:

We would appreciate your input in order to help other Dells visitors make the most of their Dells vacations. Please take a few minutes to complete the following survey, and mail to: Wisconsin Dells Guidebook, c/o Prairie Oak Press, 821 Prospect Place, Madison, WI 53703.

1. What was the name of the lodging place you stayed at on your most recent Dells visit?

_____

2. What type of establishment was it? (motel, condo, campground, etc.)

_____

3. Please rate your accommodations for each category by placing an X in the circle that best describes your feelings toward the place you stayed.

Overall lodging experience	☺	☺	☹	don't know
Cleanliness	☺	☺	☹	don't know
Pool/water recreation area	☺	☺	☹	don't know
Picnic area	☺	☺	☹	don't know
Security/feeling safe	☺	☺	☹	don't know
Children's play area	☺	☺	☹	don't know
Price/overall value	☺	☺	☹	don't know

Other comments about your lodging place:

4. For up to five restaurants you visited on your most recent Dells trip, rate each one on quality of food and service. If you particularly enjoyed a menu item and want to recommend it to others, use the space provided on the right to do so. Feel free to rate any restaurant, including carryout, fast food, and bar/grill type restaurants.

Restaurant Number 1:   Food   ☺ ☻ ☹   I'd suggest:

Name _____   Service   ☺ ☻ ☹

_____

Restaurant Number 2:   Food   ☺ ☻ ☹   I'd suggest:

Name _____   Service   ☺ ☻ ☹

_____

Restaurant Number 3:   Food   ☺ ☻ ☹   I'd suggest:

Name _____   Service   ☺ ☻ ☹

_____

Restaurant Number 4:   Food   ☺ ☻ ☹   I'd suggest:

Name _____   Service   ☺ ☻ ☹

_____

Restaurant Number 5:   Food   ☺ ☻ ☹   I'd suggest:

Name _____   Service   ☺ ☻ ☹

_____

Other comments about restaurants:

5. For up to five attractions you visited on your most recent Dells stay, rate each one by placing an X in the circle that best represents your feelings about that attraction. IMPORTANT: if more than one person wants to rate the same attraction, instead of marking a circle with an X, use A, B, C, D, etc. for each group member, and give the age and gender for each group member in the space provided.

Group Member A is a   __ Male   __Female   Age ___

Group Member B is a   __ Male   __Female   Age ___

Group Member C is a   __ Male   __Female   Age ___

Group Member D is a   __ Male   __Female   Age ___

Group Member E is a   __ Male   __Female   Age ___

Attraction Number 1:   Fun   ☺ ☺ ☹
Attraction _____   Value for price   ☺ ☺ ☹

Attraction Number 2:   Fun   ☺ ☺ ☹
Attraction _____   Value for price   ☺ ☺ ☹

Attraction Number 3:   Fun   ☺ ☺ ☹
Attraction _____   Value for price   ☺ ☺ ☹

Attraction Number 4:   Fun   ☺ ☺ ☹
Attraction _____   Value for price   ☺ ☺ ☹

Attraction Number 5:   Fun   ☺ ☺ ☹
Attraction _____   Value for price   ☺ ☺ ☹

Other comments about attractions:

Were there any retail shops that you really liked or disliked? If so feel free to make comments below. If you can't recall the name of a shop, then describe approximately where it was located or anything else you recall about it.

Is there any information not included in this book that you would suggest we include in the future?

Thank you for your comments, and for reading *The Wisconsin Dells: A Completely Unauthorized Guide.*